The
ULTIMATE
WEBSITE
PROMOTION
Handbook

by

Chris Standring

The Ultimate Website Promotion Handbook © Chris Standring 2004-2006
PO Box 1993, Studio City, CA 91614 USA
chris@aandronline.com

Published by Montserrat Publishing
5 Coverdale Road, London, NW2 4DB, England.
Tel: 07984 830 408 Fax: 020 8909 1247

Montserrat
Publishing

Cover design by Peter Sjöstedt Hughes www.graphicdesigneurope.com
Typeset by Publishing Solutions www.publishingsolutions.co.uk
Printed in Spain by MCC Graphics www.mccgraphics.co.uk
ISBN 0-9528358-3-5 / 978-0-9528358-3-7

Disclaimer
This handbook is designed to provide good reliable information regarding
the subject matter covered. However, it is distributed with the
understanding that the author is not engaged in any legal or professional
advice. The author and publishers specifically disclaim any liability that is
incurred from the use or the application of contents of this book.

Publisher's note
Please note that this amazing book is suitable for both the web-designing
fraternity and those with no computing skills whatsoever. If you are new to
the Internet world, you might like to skip some of the technical detail in
this handbook and focus more on the material relating to marketing and
attracting visitors to your site. If, on the other hand, you are already
familiar with the aesthetics side of web-design, you should read every word
of *The Ultimate Website Promotion Handbook* to learn more about the
business side and watch your or your clients' websites grow in popularity.

Contents

PART THREE Page Optimization

"Chris, thanks so much for writing *The Ultimate Website Promotion Handbook.* By following your advice, according to proper site optimization, my web site is now listed on page 1 in Google, page 2 on AllTheWeb, page 1 on Hotbot and page 1 on Yahoo for the keywords 'easy listening instrumental'. I applied the web site optimization techniques you listed in your eBook the same day I purchased it. In less than 4 weeks I've gone from not being found by any search engine to being listed in 6!

I know I would have spent hundreds of dollars to achieve the same results I obtained by following the info you gave in your book. I hope you have and will continue to have success with your music and internet businesses. Thanks again."

Anne Allen www.easylisteninganne.com

"I wish I had read Chris Standring's *The Ultimate Website Promotion Handbook* BEFORE I built my web-site. It would have saved me a bundle of time and money, not to mention sales lost due to pure ignorance of how to intelligently approach the key factors of promoting any web business.

I wasn't more than a dozen pages in when I became convinced that this book would change everything for our web business. We built a web-site that looked great, functioned well and was totally useless because no one knew we existed. I began to feel very disheartened about our internet venture. Then I read Chris' book *The Ultimate Website Promotion Handbook* and the clouds lifted. He lays out in witty, easy to follow language exactly how to optimize your site for ranking in search engines as well as tons of ideas about promoting and marketing an online business.

If you have an online business, you need this book. It will show you in a fun straight-forward way how to get the word out, if you don't have an online business, read this book – you'll want to start one immediately! *The Ultimate Website Promotion Handbook* is a treasure map, literally."

David Beeler, co-founder Beeler Greetings

"Excellent! PACKED with solid information! If I were just starting out and wanted to know how to make money online, I'd get this 90-page powerhouse and act on every tip in it!"

Dr. Joe Vitale, #1 Best-Selling Author – 'Spiritual Marketing'
www.MrFire.com

Testimonials for original online version

"A friend recommended *The Ultimate Website Promotion Handbook,* but I was a bit reluctant to read it because normally I can't be bothered with web design books. But as soon as I started reading this book, I realised it was different. I couldn't put it down and now having read it, I realise there's no point in having a beautifully designed website if nobody's seeing it. Today, all businesses need a website… and all websites need this excellent guide."

Steve Grant, Managing Director, Cititec Associates Limited, IT Recruitment for Investment Banks

"Internet Marketing books are a dime a dozen on the web – I've read enough of them to last me a lifetime. But I must say *The Ultimate Website Promotion Handbook* by Chris Standring really stood out to me. I thoroughly enjoyed reading it! As someone who literally makes their living selling music on the Internet, I can verify that Chris' techniques are dead on. If you have a product or idea you want to sell online, *The Ultimate Web Site Promotion Handbook* will put you on the fast track to setting up and running your own successful Internet business – and quick. Well done!"

David Nevue, founder of the Music Biz Academy and author of 'How to Promote Your Music Successfully on the Internet'

"Chris – Your latest eBook is absolutely amazing! I truly can't believe the specificity of the secrets you're giving away. It answers questions that I've been asking for years, only to find that the answers were closely guarded or cloaked in mystery. The book is crammed with loads of useful tips & secrets – I can't wait to apply some of them to my site! Congrats on a superbly written book."

Jim Wilson, www.jimwilson.net

"Chris, I just finished reading your book and I have to say I love it. I have my own web development company and have learned so much from your book. This is a 'must read' for anyone who's interested in improving their web presence. I plan on making *The Ultimate Web Site Promotion Handbook* required reading for my internet clients as it answers so many questions my clients always ask. Nice Job Chris... Jolly Good Old Chap!"

Dave Hooper, Lead Designer, www.hooper.com

About the author

Chris Standring is a British born recording artist presently signed to **Trippin' In Rhythm/V2 records**. He is also an Internet entrepreneur with several successful ventures including:

Play Jazz Guitar.com www.playjazzguitar.com
A website for jazz guitar enthusiasts and a vehicle to sell his home study jazz guitar course *"Play What You Hear"*.

Guitar Made Simple www.guitarmadesimple.com
A website for beginner guitarists and a vehicle to sell his home study beginners/intermediate guitar course *"Guitar Made Simple"*.

A &R Online www.aandronline.com
A website dedicated to hooking up independent artists with the music industry and a vehicle to sell his educational music biz eBooks and affiliate products.

Chris Standring.com www.chrisstandring.com
His personal fan site where visitors can view tour schedule, buy CDs and so on.

Introduction

I have to be honest. There's a big part of me that doesn't want you to read this handbook. Now I know to some of you that might sound like some typical Hollywood marketing nonsense, but I am very serious when I say this. After all, you have already bought this book so it's not like I need to sell you on it anymore. The fact of the matter is I have spent the last few years thinking about writing this book and every time I pondered the idea I came up with resistance. Resistance from close friends who saw what I was doing and resistance from myself. *"Why should I give all my secrets away?"* seemed to be the response everywhere. *"What if others figure it out, duplicate these ideas and put me out of business?"* These were very real thoughts, and very real arguments to justify not writing. And so I didn't, and everything was safe for a while.

So why have I decided all of a sudden to spill the beans? Because I know deep down there are so many online businesses out there NOT competing with mine, why not give a little? I figure I am ahead of the game and there is no reason to stop being ahead of the game.

The other reason I have decided to write this is that I have absolutely no interest in being hired as a search engine optimizer, or a web designer for that matter. None whatsoever. I did it on the side for a short while to make some extra cash and frankly it was a drag. I have no interest to maintain other people's websites. They want them updated weekly and most want it done for free. Not for me. Besides I am too busy with my own Internet ventures to have time to perfect others. Because I am not interested in being a freelance consultant in these areas, I am not killing a business for myself. Now on the other hand, all those professional search engine optimizers out there who would otherwise take thousands of pounds from you to get you top rankings, well they may have a real problem with me right now, and who can blame them? But honestly, I like to play the guitar. I'd still rather do that than personally optimize websites for people. So I thought I'd show you exactly how *you* can! You know that old saying, "You can give a man a fish and feed him for a day, and you can give a man a fishing rod and he'll eat for a lifetime?" Think of this handbook as your fishing rod. If you follow my ideas to the letter, you'll be eating well for quite some time.

Finally, I decided to write this course because I am hoping lots of people will buy it. That would make me very happy. Oh… and my girlfriend too!

Everything you read in this course has been put into practice with amazing results. Each one of my websites currently enjoys page 1 rankings on Google.com and as a result, I sell many products daily on the Internet. If you follow these ideas to the letter, there is no reason why you cannot achieve the same. In fact I guarantee you will. There are two important steps: 1) page layout and optimization and 2) power linking. Neither one will work for maximum results without the other. We are going to go over each subject in depth as well as other traffic generating ideas. I wish you the very best. Feel free to contact me at **chris@aandronline.com** I would love you to share your success stories.

PART ONE

Getting Started

Links to resources

Throughout this course there are many links pointing to external resources. Some links point to software programmes that are absolutely necessary to your online business and other links point to programmes that might simply ease the load. There is no getting around doing the work but it sure helps to know what's out there that makes life easier. I have had personal experience with most of the resources that I recommend. With this in mind, feel free to hunt around for any new programme or resource that works for you.

Why do it all yourself?

OK, you could go to a website designer and have him build a site for you. He or she may well do a wonderful job. Chances are that your web designer knows nothing about the art of search engine optimization so you will have to take your finished website to a professional optimizer and expect to have much of it changed to get it to respond well in search engines. This could cost several thousand pounds. Now, on the other hand, what if you invested a little time and hard work and learned both of these very attainable procedures yourself?

The upside to learning yourself is this: low cost and the ability to maintain your site regularly as and when you need to, without having to make phone calls to your webmaster hounding them to get a site updated. The incentive is all yours to learn and I strongly recommend you do so. You can buy html authoring software at a reasonable price. I personally use *Dreamweaver* (**www.dreamweaver.com**), as it is considered the professional's choice. I would recommend you learn to write html code at least to a basic level. There are many software programmes that incorporate WYSIWYG (what you see is what you get). Web pages are generated by a very simple code and when these WYSIWYG programmes mess up (something that happens quite often), the only way to fix it is to go into the source code and repair it by hand. That is my experience anyway. I am sure there are arguments against this as there are plenty of successful webmasters who have not learned html but speaking personally, there is never a problem I can't fix now regarding html code, simply because I know how it works.

I would recommend buying *Dreamweaver* because you can split the screen so you can view page design at the bottom half of the page and source code at the top half of the page. This is also a great way to learn html as you can see exactly how adding elements to your design generates code and vice versa.

Another html programme I used sometime ago was *CoffeeCup HTML Editor* (**www.coffeecup.com**). This is another first class software company who, like *Dreamweaver,* tends to stay ahead of the curve. It is also considerably cheaper. Personally I would go for Dreamweaver every time as I think it is the best on the market. But hey that's just me.

There are many books you can buy and you might consider picking one up to have at hand. Here's one: *Learn HTML in a Weekend* by Steve Callihan. (you can find this by searching on **www.amazon.co.uk**). Honestly, I never bought an html 'how to' book but instead looked up anything that I didn't understand on the Internet. Trial and error is always best. *Dreamweaver* has a built in html help file, which was a help to me back when I started.

And if you don't want to do it yourself…

…then of course feel free to hire someone to make your website for you. Many folks just don't have the time or the inclination. However, there is something you simply must understand: it is one thing to design a nice looking website, but it is quite another to design it and optimize it so it will perform well from a marketing and promotional standpoint. If you decide to outsource your web design, it is critical that you work alongside your designer so that he or she understands everything discussed in this handbook. The role of a search engine optimizer and Internet marketer is quite different from a web designer.

FTP software

You will need to get some FTP software. FTP stands for File Transfer Protocol. Essentially it is a very simple programme that enables you to upload your website files to your server space. I use *CuteFTP* (**www.cuteftp.com**) and I highly recommend it. Another popular one is *WS_FTP* (**www.wsftp.com**).

Make sure you upload your main page as **index.html** as this will be the default page when someone types in **www.yoursite.com**.

Alrighty, let's get to some nitty gritty….

What sells on the Internet and what does not?

So you want to start a business on the Internet? More importantly, the question to ask is: "Do you want to have a *successful* business on the Internet?" Well that sounds like a dumb question, right? Not really, because thousands of ambitious folks are starting Internet ventures on a daily basis and most of them, probably over 90%, don't know what is ahead of them and have not researched enough to put themselves on the right track. Many don't even have a business model. Several years ago (remember the dot com boom?) venture capitalists poured millions of pounds into web start ups that had absolutely no idea how they were going to generate income. It just seemed like a good idea at the time. And so, unsurprisingly, these start-ups became 'end-ups' within a very short amount of time.

That was then. This is now. Many folks have learned that in order to have a successful business, you must have something marketable to sell, a focused business model, and now there are many success stories and profitable websites as a result. Many of these are one man/woman organisations making thousands of pounds monthly, but it pays to get it right from the start. I have spent six years perfecting my online business, keeping up to date with search engine changes (seeing search engine algorithms effect my rankings – positively and negatively!) and I believe I can show you how to have exactly the same success that I currently enjoy online.

The first subject you have to understand before you delve into an online business is to know what products will sell and what will not. Personally I am only interested in starting a website that will make money. Although I enjoy writing and offering information, I expect to be paid well to do it. That said, there are many things that one should offer others for "free" in order to seduce them to the credit card server. But, for the most part, I am interested in profiting from any website I start. And with that I won't be discussing how to promote a website dedicated to saving whales, as wonderful creatures as they may be!

The first thing to understand is that what may sell in a store front on your local high street may not sell at all on the Internet. People who go on the Internet are usually looking for something specific. They are mostly looking for information, wanting to research or learn more about something in particular. The Internet is essentially a huge library of information. This is why search engines are so necessary. Aside from information, the other thing that people are looking for on the Internet is bargains. They might be looking to buy a specific item and will go online to see if they can get it cheaper. Thirdly, people will shop and buy products online that they don't necessarily need to speak to a sales rep about. For instance, people book travel online. They don't need to speak to a sales rep to know more about that product as they already know that they just want to get from A to B, usually via the cheapest method. So they shop for flight tickets online. Same with hotels and rental cars. Now travel websites are so thorough you can click on photos and see what the hotel room looks like, view prices etc. You don't need a sales rep to walk you through that. People buy books and music online. They know exactly what they are and don't need a sales rep. They are confident that they will be able to read the books and the CDs will fit into their stereo systems.

Let's talk about what may NOT do quite so well on the Internet...

If you were looking for a coffee table to buy, you might want to go into a store, look at a few and get some help from a sales rep to learn more about them. You might want to physically feel one or two of them. Would you do a search for "coffee tables" on the Internet and click to buy? No I didn't think you would. You might search around to get ideas, but probably not buy online. However, if you owned a store on the high street you might want to have a website displaying information and photos about your coffee tables you have on sale in your showroom. The point is that selling coffee tables is not an online business in itself. It does not exist 100% on the Internet. It needs the traditional bricks and mortar model for it to work.

So the biggest question you should ask yourself is:

"Would someone be *searching* for my product on the Internet?"

Remember:

- **Information**
- **Bargains**
- **Products that don't need a sales rep**

Let's talk a bit more about #1: **Information.** As a sole Internet entrepreneur, I think this is probably the most successful avenue on which to model your business. You can sell information on the web. If you are an expert in a given field, you can write articles and eBooks and write a regular newsletter that you send to subscribers. You can even charge money to your subscribers if there is value.

The more passionate and knowledgeable you are on a given subject the more successful you will be!

This format is my personal favourite because I am a huge fan of automating everything. When you sell an eBook online you are making 100% profit. There are no manufacturing costs and best of all, you never run out of books! Lastly, whenever you sell an eBook you get an E-mail confirming a sale and you don't need to do a thing. No shipping, no manufacturing, no warehousing storage and so on. It's a 24 hour business that completely runs itself. You will work hard setting up everything to run smoothly and of course you will have to write your eBook, but once the work is done, it runs itself. Your time from then on should be spent promoting your website. I'll get to that soon.

Search term suggestions

OK. Let's talk more about choosing a product and finding out whether it will work successfully online. Keep in mind the big question, *"Who is searching for this product?".* If we can ascertain whether or not a product has a life on the web before we set out to promote it, we can save ourselves a great deal of grief. There is a fabulous tool called the *Overture Search Term Suggestion Tool,* which is invaluable if you are looking to start an online business. You can type in a keyword and it will return a list of similar keywords, all ranked by order of popularity, and will give you the number of times that keyword has been searched on during that month. Bookmark this URL and use it:

http://inventory.overture.com/d/searchinventory/suggestion

Let's take a look at some keywords and see how they rank.

Count	Search Term
90580	web site promotion
283868	Internet marketing
102	website marketing success
3821678	music
98948	jazz
15258	jazz music
35	new jazz music
10661	carpet cleaner
46	carpet stain cleaner
1656355	flowers
231452	flower delivery

Bear in mind that if you search on these words the counts will vary monthly but the numbers above will do very nicely to illustrate some points. The first search term "website promotion" gets 90580 counts. This means that this amount of people have done searches on the phrase *website promotion* during one month. "Internet marketing" gets 283868 counts, clearly more popular. "Website marketing success" only gets 102 counts. This should tell you that you should not target your site for this keyword-phrase. (No hang on, I should tell myself that!).

"Music" gets a whopping 3821678 searches a month. "Jazz" gets 98948 and jazz music gets a lower 15258. "New jazz music" only gets 35 counts! Yikes!! Does this mean no one is interested in new jazz music? Not necessarily. They just wouldn't use that keyword to find it. Same with "carpet stain cleaner". They would search on "carpet cleaner".

This suggestion tool helps a great deal. Clearly the one word keywords are most popular but they are more difficult to optimize your website with because of bigger competition. It will be very hard to optimize your website for the keyword "music" but a great deal easier to target "jazz music". The search term suggestion tool tells you that there is still a good amount of searches for the phrase "jazz music" and it is much more specific. This also tells you that you should not start a website targeting your main keyword phrase "Carpet stain cleaner". You will clearly have a garage full of product (but possibly a very clean carpet!). On the other hand, if your website was **www.carpetstaincleaner.com**, you might get lucky as people might find your site when they do a search on "carpet cleaner". It's all down to how you optimize the rest of the web page as the words "carpet" and "cleaner" both exist in the phrase "carpet stain cleaner". You understand? Head trip yet? I hope not. Deep breathing time. And rest... ok....

The trick is finding *two or three word* key phrases making sure that those keywords are actually being searched. A two or three word phrase is much more specific, more relevant to the user and easier to optimize. Everyone wins. Take some time deciding on the right keyword using the *Overture* search term suggestion tool; it will make all the difference to your future web traffic. When you have got some ideas, write them down and then go to **www.netsol.com** and see if they are available as domain names. You can get suggestions for other domain names too from the same website.

**It is extremely important that your main keyword phrase
you are targeting is part of your domain name!**

Choosing Your Domain Name

You've decided exactly what your website is going to be all about. You know what product you intend to sell and the next step is to buy a domain name. Getting this step right is absolutely crucial.

Google.com is now the most popular search engine by far with whom all other search engines are now competing. Some time ago I was having huge Google success with web pages which did not contain a keyword within its domain name. For instance, I have a very popular music site featuring unsigned artists at **www.aandronline.com**. I tried an experiment in the early days as an affiliate with a travel company. Instead of starting a new site called **www.hotels-something-or-other.com** I simply created a sub folder at aandronline.com with the URL: **www.aandronline.com/hotels/**. The site was (and still is) geared to selling hotels in Las Vegas. During 2002 I was averaging 2,700 visits per day, sometimes booking well over 20 hotel reservations daily. My commission cheques were anywhere between £2,000 and £6,000 monthly – for that affiliate only! That was a lovely thing I can tell you. Then, December of that year, I checked my stats one day and saw that traffic had gone down to less than 100 visits per day. My #1 ranked keywords "Hotels in Las Vegas" and "Las Vegas hotels" were relegated to page 7 in Google's index. My heart sunk as you can imagine. I received a cheque that month from that affiliate company for under £100.00. I was devastated (and so were they!!) So of course I went straight to work trying to resurrect my rankings.

Over the months I learned what had happened. *Google* was no longer interested in my travel sub folder at a music website. In its eyes it was no longer relevant. It had changed its rules and thousands upon thousands of websites had lost business as a result. What happened? Google decided that it was to take top level domains much more seriously along with link popularity. My sub folder travel directory had lost rankings to top level domains like **www.lasvegas.com** or **www.lasvegashotels.com** or **www.vegas.com** and quite rightly. I was simply messing around experimenting, getting lucky. These top level sites were corporate businesses, up until that point competing with ME! The Google change made sense, I just didn't like it. Later, I got business back with **www.hotelchain.net** and targeted a couple of easier keywords with huge success. However, I have to say that since my music sites now take up all my time, I have let this site go.

That said, things are constantly changing. At the time of this writing, it is extremely possible to have great success with a website that simply has a branded name without keywords existing within a domain name. Several websites come to mind: **www.taxi.com** (a music website), **www.fool.com** (a stock market & finance website) and **www.amazon.com** (books & music etc).

The upside to getting a keyword rich domain name is that when other sites link back to you, your keyword resides in what is called 'anchor text', the text that contains the link to your site. This anchor text is all important to search engines. More on this later.

So the moral of this story? Let's get you the right domain name right now before you go and do something wrong. We have talked about *Overture's* search term suggestion tool. I suggest you decide on ONE killer main keyword phrase, two secondary keywords and build your main page around that. Let's take an example: Montana fly fishing. At this precise moment of writing I have found **www.montanaflyfishing.com** and www.montana-fly-fishing.com. Both of which don't come up on Google's 1st page of search results when I type in "Fly fishing in Montana". That tells me that if I bought www.montana-fly-fishing.net (which at the time of this writing IS still available), I could optimize that page, power link it (to be discussed in a while) and beat the hell out of everyone! Anyone who owns those top level domains could be raking in the money. They just don't know how.

I have also learned quite recently that if you want to start a website all about American history, for example, you could buy the domain www.americanhistory.com OR www.american-history.com and get results just as effectively. The hyphen "-" between words will not hinder search engine results. Similarly, you can get different extensions like .net or .org or .cc or .biz or .tv and so on and have similar success. I like to stick to .com if I can get it but it has become increasingly hard as more and more keywords get bought. However, I find that I can usually get what I want with a little creativity. My business is 100% online so I need that keyword phrase in my domain name. I can't call my website *"Chris' brilliant Internet ideas"*. Why? Because www.chris-brilliant-internet-ideas.com is going to get diddlysquat when people search for any of my products in the search engines.

The other thing to think about when purchasing a domain name is that if you choose a .net or .org etc., you run the risk of sending traffic to a .com. If you have www.cookiesandcakes.net and a visitor wants to return to your site after a couple of months, he or she may type in www.cookiesandcakes.com instead, potentially giving business to a competitor. Try to get a .com first and work from there.

Another very real situation is this: you may have an existing bricks and mortar company that you want to take to the web but the already branded name doesn't contain a keyword. For example, you have a family flower delivery business that is firmly established and has been in business 30 years. Let's say the business is called Flashman Hillard & Co. There are two ways to proceed. First you create a whole new keyword-laden domain name, something like flower-delivery.com (or similar). You then promote that domain everywhere on the web. Next you buy a second domain called www.flashmanhillard.com and redirect that website to flower-delivery.com. Anytime you want to promote offline through traditional advertising, you can give people your existing brand name as they will get redirected to your site anyway. The second idea would be to incorporate your existing brand name amongst a keyword phrase such as **www.FlashmanFlowerDelivery.com** and then promote that. The choice is yours.

As I have mentioned, there are many successful websites that have flourished without having a keyword in their domain name. However, search engines update their algorithms constantly which means that at any time they may bring extra relevance to a keyword domain name. But most importantly, as we will discuss later, promoting your website is a lot easier if you do include a keyword. You'll see when we get to that a little later.

Registering your domain name and finding a reliable web host

Splendid. You have decided on a good domain name and you're ready for action. There are a couple of different avenues to take at this point. First I would recommend that you register your domain at *Network Solutions* (**www.netsol.com**). This is the most trusted Internet registration organization and I would recommend that you register there. Registering a domain name at network solutions will cost around £40 for 3 years. Personally I would rather pay this than less anywhere else. I don't know whether a little company will be around to give me any support if I need it in the future. With Network Solutions I feel comfortable. However, if you feel more at ease registering with a UK company, I have friends back home who recommend *UKreg* (**www.ukreg.com**).

The other way to go is to have your web host register for you. You will need a reliable web hosting company to host your website and very often when you purchase one of their hosting programmes they will take care of domain registration for you. I don't recommend this though.

There is no getting around web hosting. You simply have to have it and you need more than a "one page" hosted at *Network Solutions*. You will need a good amount of space (depending on the amount and size of files you are uploading) and a web host that includes several features certainly wouldn't hurt. By features, I mean additional freebies such as: statistics & logs, CGI scripts, (necessary for contact web forms etc.), and so on.

If you decide to go through **www.netsol.com** to register your domain, you will need to manually change your DNS server settings. This basically tells *Network Solutions* that your domain name needs to point towards the web host server that you designate. To change these settings is a very simple procedure. Once you sign up with your new web host, you will get an E-mail with their DNS settings. Simply login to your Network Solutions account and click on "Go directly to account manager" select your account and click on "edit DNS". Then simply add the new DNS server settings and submit. Ta-dah!

As far as reliable hosting companies are concerned, I would strongly recommend the following:they are all extremely professional with great technical support and their fees won't burn a hole in your pocket.

TotalChoiceHosting **www.totalchoicehosting.com**
HostRocket.com **www.hostrocket.com**

The above companies are based in the USA but, if you prefer, feel free to hunt around in the UK for a good reliable and inexpensive host. Many are extremely competitive these days, so it shouldn't be hard to find a bargain.

Your product or affiliate

There are two ways to make great money on the Internet:

1) By inventing your own product and selling it on your website
2) By selling someone else's product through an affiliate link on your website.

Selling your own product is by far the most fulfilling as you are marketing an invention of your own. Let's say you live in Montana and write a book on fly fishing. You target "fly fishing" as your key phrase or "Montana fly fishing" for an easier compete. You convert your document to an eBook and sell it over the net. You start a newsletter, offer it to subscribers once a month and advertise your eBook in that newsletter. 100% of the revenue goes to you (save a few pennies to your merchant account credit card company). Lovely.

Selling a product through an affiliate link is rewarding too but not as much, as far as I'm concerned. Basically it goes like this: your "Fly Fishing In Montana" website is set up to sell your eBook, but over the months you see traffic increase as well as your subscriber base. Why not sell fishing rods and tackle? Anything to do with fishing for that matter. You could find a dealer online, sign up on their affiliate programme where they give you a unique URL to link to, and you have an instant cash generating source.

OK. Enough about fishing. I haven't done it since I was 14!

Personally I like to use affiliate programmes as "gravy" rather than the main focus of my website, although there are plenty of online affiliates making thousands of pounds monthly from this source alone. Actually, come to think of it, one of my earliest money spinners on the Internet was made up of affiliate income exclusively. **www.hotelchain.net** was a place where you could find and book travel related stuff anywhere in the world. The site was affiliated with four different online companies who dealt with all the back end reservation stuff so you could find a hotel, flight or rental car anywhere worldwide. I simply made the search engine friendly web pages so people could find my site first.

To look for an appropriate affiliate programme, do a web search on "Affiliate Programmes" and look for something that appeals to you. It's always free to sign up once you choose a product and usually takes a couple of minutes to get your affiliate link. Stay away from low commissions. I like big priced items that I can make around 30 to 40% commission on. Selling cheap items making 50 pence per sale does nothing to stimulate my interest I have to say. I like to make around £15.00 plus in commission, before I commit to any affiliate programme. Having said that, I'll work hard to make that commission. More on that later.

You might decide to sell a physical product over the Internet; music or books let's say. Perhaps a home study course on a DVD. This is all fine but understand one thing:

> **Product fulfillment = work**
> **Downloadable information = play**

If you sell a physical product, there is a great deal more work to do. Let's say you have a music CD to sell. There are manufacturing costs, recording costs, artwork etc. Then when an order comes in you have to bag it up and ship it. You can of course charge a shipping fee but there is still a business to monitor carefully. If you are selling 30 CDs daily over the Internet, it might be very difficult to go away on holiday without someone looking after your orders. Of course this is a very nice problem to have but if you are selling downloadable files you can take a few days off knowing that everything is probably OK. You might want to grab your e-mail every morning while you're gone to make sure the ship is running, you know delete some spam, that kind of thing.

Why have a website?

There are two main reasons to have a website: first, to start a dedicated online business and sell products and/or information: second, to use as a calling card. You may have an existing bricks & mortar high street shop selling garden furniture. When you meet someone on a business trip or at a party who is interested in patio chairs, you can send them to your website. From there, they can browse photos of things you sell in your store and they can contact you directly.

Sometimes I ask people why they want to start a website. Many say, "Because everyone has one". This might seem like a justifiable reason but I don't agree. I say let's put it to use. It's a fabulous marketing tool and something that we can control. I have spent the last twenty odd years as a professional musician. I have seen the music business change and go through some odd times. I never liked the fact that much of the business can be out of a musician's control. I would be somewhat reliant on a phone call to be offered a gig, or a record company doing their job promoting at retail, or a radio station adding my new single so I can market my new CD in that territory. I don't like that level of uncontrollability anymore. I dealt with it for many years but now I am in my 40s, I am not interested in sitting and waiting for stuff to happen.

The powerful thing about the Internet is that so much of it IS in our control. I am now as successful as I put in the hours to be. I have a successful Internet business promoting not only informational products (eBooks on how to market music etc.) but I also sell CDs from my own website and fans of my music show up to my gigs because I can personally let them know when and where I am performing, if they subscribe to my mailing list.

So we either have a website because it is a business online or we have a website to complement our traditional business offline. I am going to assume for the sake of this course that you are interested in fully promoting your online business as a dedicated 100% *let's-make-all-the-dough-we-can-because-I-hate-my-job* Internet venture.

Now from here on out, if we are going to make the most of the Internet, our website is going to ostensibly serve two purposes and only two purposes:

- **Sell products**
- **Collect e-mail addresses** (so we can sell products directly)

Anything else on your website should be clever seduction to get visitors to buy your products or give you their e-mail address. Now this might seem ruthless and cold but it should not manifest that way online. After all, a visitor will usually only buy a product from you if they trust you. You will need to gain respect as an expert in your field and offer money back guarantees and have testimonials supporting your products. Simple ways to get visitors to give you their e-mail address might be: "Click here to get more information" and have them contact you with a question. Or a newsletter offering information on a regular basis or a members only zone where they need to input a name and e-mail address. If you offer substance, you can expect intrigue. When you have intrigue, folks will give up an e-mail address. When you get an e-mail address you can parlay that into sales. I'll show you how. Stick with me....

Make your website attractive, exciting and fun to visit!

Mini-marketing product sites versus portals

Here are a couple of ideas for you to think about regarding selling your product. Let's say you have an eBook you want to sell called *"Break Your Fear Of Public Speaking"*. There are two ways you could go with this: the first way is to start a mini-website and get a domain that includes the key phrase *"speaking-in-public"* or *"public-speaking-something-or-other"* .com etc. (depending what is available – make sure that your domain name includes the two keywords *speaking* and *public):* next, you make a one page sales letter with all the glitz, glamour and marketing hype that is necessary to seduce people to enter their credit card info, and you optimize that web page, power link it and send it into cyberspace. When people enter your keywords in a search engine, your page hopefully comes up high on the first page of results and you sell them your eBook. Your website is straight to the point. No messing. The intention is clear: Buy my book!

The second way to go might be to start a website that has more of a community feel about it. Not only can they buy your eBook but you might have a discussion forum where those with a fear of public speaking can join together in quiet desperation. You might also have a few affiliate links to other eBooks you recommend. You would trade links with other sites to get traffic and start a regular e-newsletter for subscribers. Of course in your newsletter you would advertise your eBook and increase your percentage of sales.

There is no right or wrong way to go. The mini-site is popular and it gets to the point. The major-site, however, enables you to expand a subscriber base and sell future products. They say in marketing that repeat customers are everything. I like the large site personally but have had success with mini-sites. When I go to a mini-site I sometimes feel like I am being sold hard on something and they don't really care about me. Do they really need to care? Well no they don't but if I feel like they don't, I subconsciously might think I'm being taken for a ride. I am hard to sell to. If I buy something on line, I want to know all about it. I will research, I will find out what others say about it and will probably have a couple of questions to e-mail tech support about before I buy. Can I get this assurance from a mini site? Maybe not. The sales pitch better be bloody good. The choice is yours.

PART TWO

Building the Website

Website design

It goes without saying that a professional looking website is going to get you more respect, and visitors will take you more seriously than if you have a poorly designed one. I know for me, when I visit other people's websites, I want to see things that are neat and orderly, a site that loads quickly and is navigated easily. I am frustrated when I have to constantly click on the back browser button to get back to a main menu. With this in mind, I am going to spend some time explaining what I feel is a good effective website, how to lay out your pages and how to link them correctly so not only your visitors are happy but so are the search engine spiders.

First we need to talk a little bit about programmes that help with illustration. Whilst it is possible to make web pages that are purely html, at some point it is nice to have a photo or company logo. Essentially, we need programmes that help us make circles! Your html authoring web design programme doesn't know how to do that yet. We need help from programmes that help us draw circles, create logos, layer colours and manipulate images. Enter a good paint programme....

Paint programmes

Adobe Photoshop is the industry standard when it comes to paint programmes. It enables you to make images, manipulate photographs, design logos and headings and more. This programme is extremely deep and I have to say I understand just a tiny bit of what it is really capable of. However, as far as I am concerned, I need Photoshop for just a couple of things. Firstly, if I have a photograph I have scanned, I need to manipulate that photo and reduce its size to make it fit on my web page. I might want to brighten it or change it from black & white to a sepia tone. Secondly, I might want to make a groovy logo like this:

Computer users usually have a limited amount of fonts set on their computers. This means that if I specify an unusual font name in my html page, I can't guarantee that everyone will have that font. In fact, the chances are they won't. The best way to make sure that everyone sees your page the same way, if you want to use a groovy font, is to make headings and logos in a paint programme such as *Photoshop*. (All computers are set up with basic fonts such as Times New Roman, Ariel, Verdana etc.). The programme allows you to make image background colours correspond seamlessly with html backgrounds using web colour codes.

Of course *Photoshop* is a little pricey! Around £350. You could start off with a smaller graphics programme if you require minimal use. You might try *Paint Shop Pro* (**www.jasc.com**) by a company called *Jasc*. I started off with this back in the early days and I found it to be an exceptional programme. It certainly does not have the capabilities of Photoshop but if it is just images and logos you need, then I would highly recommend this programme. It is a very affordable £60 or so.

Whichever programme you decide to use, you will be saving your image files as **.jpg** or **.gif** in order to upload them to the web. Make sure that your image files are small in order for page loading to be kept to a minimum. If I go to a website and a page takes more than a few seconds to load, I close it! I leave immediately. I have no patience. I think it is safe to assume that most net surfers are now just as impatient and you should design your pages with this in mind. Keep your graphics to a minimum! If you want to display a full size photo, then make a text link or a thumbnail image that when clicked on takes visitors to a new window with the full size photo. That way, once your large photo is viewed, visitors can close out that window and return to your menu.

Flash versus HTML

Flash (**www.flash.com**) is a popular movie animation programme compatible with html. Here's some inside information for you:

Search engines cannot spider flash animation!

If you have a splash page (an introduction page that says something like *"Welcome to Jonathan's Ice Cream Parlour, step right in, click here to enter"*) and the splash page is 100% flash animated with whirring ice cream cones darting across the page with no html static text, you can forget high search engine rankings. If there are no other websites dedicated to different flavours of Ice Cream, then, providing you have a good domain name, you may or may not get lucky when someone types in "Ice Cream". Frankly, I would hazard a guess that you would stay buried amongst the rubble of other poorly optimized websites. By the way, do try to avoid selling ice cream over the web! Might be a sticky process!

Flash is a fun, snappy, impressive medium that designers have a field day with. I must say I personally have a pet peeve with flash sites. They annoy the heck out of me. I am usually looking for information when I do a search, or trying to find a quick answer to a problem. I don't want to spend five minutes being entertained by an animator in order to get the information I need. Perhaps I sound like an old curmudgeon but there we are.

Flash has its place though. When used sparingly, I think it has a profound effect. The great thing about flash is that you can integrate a flash file within an html web page and still optimize the page for search engines. Bear in mind that flash animation takes up page loading time and you don't want to lose anyone. I love the idea of flash animated short movies providing I have the choice whether to view them or not.

Search engines can only spider *static text!*

If you have a web page that is entirely flash driven, then essentially you have imported a movie file into your web page, something that a search engine doesn't understand. It sees the file name but that's all it sees. Your main index page should contain mostly static text with a couple of graphic images optimized with the right keywords and saved as a .html extension. If you want that page found on *Google*, then any flash files should be included within the walls of your website. Let's get the search engines spidering your index page first. After all, the whole idea is to be found amongst 10 billion other websites, right?

Dynamic script pages

Many web companies hire specialists to programme their websites using dynamic script. Very often this is necessary if a huge database of information is involved. Active server pages (files with extension **.asp**) and **.php** scripting often cause search engines to spider ineffectively. Spiders need to see static html. A static html page is a file with a **.html** or **.htm** extension which is uploaded on to a server and sits there permanently until somebody goes in and physically deletes it. Active data driven pages are not static and therefore don't really exist in a tangible form as far as the search engine is concerned. They are kind of instantly produced when a script calls for them to be written. Now that said, active scripting is very often necessary (don't ask me how to do it – I haven't a clue!), depending on the nature of the website. Any type of online reservation booking or credit card server form relies heavily on active pages.

If your index page has a .asp or .php extension, I would advise changing this for good search engine optimization. Now technically, these active pages can be indexed but as they are not static, you may find competitor sites flying past you in *Google's* results. What I suggest is that you have an index page saved as a **.html** extension and optimized as necessary and then you link to your active pages from there. Another effective method is to have a reservation or search box embedded into your html page that calls your active server pages. Of course, if you are designing a web page all about fly fishing in Montana, you can ignore this extremely boring paragraph. (I know I promised I would drop the fly fishing thing!)

Frames or no frames

Frames are essentially several pages that fit within a web page called a frameset. A few years ago they were extremely popular as it made navigation of a website very easy. For example, there might be a menu with links placed in the left frame and anytime you clicked on a link from that frame, the URL would display in the right frame. It meant that you didn't have to keep making web pages with a menu on the left side of the page.

The problems all began when websites with frames looked so bad. Aesthetically it was all so unappealing. But that wasn't the main problem. The big predicament was with the search engines. They wouldn't index them. Why not? Because they didn't know what to index. Was it the left frame or the right frame? Or was it the main frame that the left frame and the right frame exist in? Well, if the main frame (the frameset) was correctly optimized with title and description, the search engines might have found it more easily. However, that was rarely done and even if it was, it might not have made any difference because there is never body text in a frameset to spider. The frameset simply calls on the left frame and the right frame to be displayed.

Anyway, to make a head trip feel well, less like a head trip, search engines eventually got it together. However, as far as you are concerned, frames are still NOT the way to go. They do not get optimized as successfully as one page with everything perfectly organized. If you insist on using frames, I strongly suggest that you have them deep within your website where it does not matter if they are found through a search engine or not. Perhaps a Members' Area, which can only be accessed through a username and password, might be appropriate. I'll give you two examples: I have a very popular website called **www.PlayJazzGuitar.com**. When anyone types in "jazz guitar" or "jazz guitar lessons" or "play jazz" or "how to play jazz guitar", my site comes up as a page 1 ranking on *Google*. Now, within that site I have a members' only zone. Visitors enter their name and e-mail address and get an autoresponder with a login and password to gain access to the members' area. The members' area is basically a frameset with a few different sub headings. It's extremely convenient to do this as each article displays in the right frame and you never lose sight of your menu links. Also, because I already have the member's e-mail address, I don't need this section to be found via search engines. You can view it here:

http://www.playjazzguitar.com/members_XX007/
Your username is: jazz your password is: fretboard

The other example is at **www.aandronline.com**, my other music website. I have a reading room where artists can pore over articles about the music business, read interviews and get ideas on how to market their music independently. This reading room does not need to be indexed (even though it probably is by now) as I have seduced visitors from my main page already. Do a search on "record deals" "how to get a record deal" or "copyright songs" or "get signed" and you will see www.aandronline.com as a page 1 *Google* ranking. It's a beautiful thing.

The other problem with frames is that they are hard to bookmark. When you bookmark a frameset, you may not be bookmarking the page that you want. You are probably bookmarking the original frameset main menu and not a page that you might have found deep within that frameset.

So, frames. Much like flash and active server pages; feel free to use them but seduce your visitors TO them from static html optimized web pages.

Page layout

Let's talk a little bit about how you might lay out your web page. Firstly, I should probably say that I am not a graphic designer by any means. My knowledge of illustration and graphic programmes is limited at best and I am to this day frightened to learn the *Flash* animation programme. It all seems so daunting. What I *do* know how to do at a professional level is put together html web pages. I know how to make them look good. I know they look good because I get e-mails from visitors telling me so and frankly it's a lot easier to believe them! I have also learned how to put together aesthetically pleasing pages that respond well in search engines and we are going to talk about this in detail. I am going to talk about effective design to a basic level. Once you can make a simple layout look good, you can experiment any way you like.

Background colours & images

Most professionally designed websites have white backgrounds. It took me quite some time to come to this realization. Visitors will feel comfortable purchasing from what they perceive is a legitimate company and because I want them to buy from me, I will always give my web page a white background. Now, that is not to say that you can't have coloured tables, rows and columns, it just means that your main body background should be white and your text should be black. I have no doubt that there will be some web designers who will argue, *"I have a black background with white text and my site is slammin!"* Well I won't argue with them but personally I think that coloured backgrounds just look amateurish to me. I am not crazy about background images either. You know, where you see a company logo duplicated 50 times with text on top. I don't like this because again, I think it looks semi pro. I've never seen a site with a background image that looked amazing to me. Besides the obvious design flaw, it adds to page loading time, and again you can't afford to turn potential customers away.

Font sizes

I think your main body text size should be medium. Most web pages are usually designed with one of three fonts; Times New Roman, Ariel or Verdana. It is safe to assume that all computers have these fonts. If you use Times font, your medium size font setting = 3. Ariel = 2 and Verdana = 2. It is safe to assume that most computer users have their font size set to medium. Headings of course can be larger. I like Verdana font personally and tend to use it a good deal. I think it looks very professional. Headings using Verdana with bold type and size=3 always look very good to me.

Working with tables

Without wishing to offer a detailed html lesson, because quite frankly you will need to explore what works best for you, I want to show you a really simple and effective way to lay out a web page. Bear in mind that once you finalize your initial main page design, you can use it as a template for all your web pages. Firstly, you are going to make a table with two columns like this:

Text with links goes here	Image logo goes here

Notice I have added a "border=1" above just so you can see the table. Your image logo (designed in Photoshop or other paint programme) can go in the right column and you might add some important text links in the left column. Now, if you take the border away, add a background colour, add a logo and text links, it might look something like this:

Home | Subscribe | Order   *Chinese Astrology*

OK, so now you have a heading that can stay on every web page within your site. This is important to unify your design throughout. The next thing is to add another table underneath for your main menu links and body text. You will add another table with 2 columns.

Home | Subscribe | Order

Chinese Astrology

Text link #1
Text link #2
Text link #3
Text link #4
Text link #5
Text link #6
Text link #7
Text link #8

Chinese astrology by Martha Hockingsworth

The foundation of Chinese Astrology is from Ying-Yang and Five Elements, which are Metal, Water, Wood, Fire and Earth. We hope you can find the Chinese Astrology secrets of you and your family's members and wish your family live luckier, wealthier, healthier, happier and longer.

Rat Ox Tiger Rabbit Dragon Snake Horse Goat Monkey Rooster Dog Pig

So now you can add all your menu text links in the left column and your body text in the right column, like this:

The more text you put in the columns the more the tables will be pushed down. This is very convenient. All that is left to do is to compose the substance of the website. This is extremely basic design as I mentioned but, when we come on to discuss optimization for search engines, the simpler the better. I will explain why when we get to it.

Content is king

For some bizarre reason *Google* seems to know the difference between real substance and faked keyword placed content. I believe that if you are indeed an expert in your field, then the first thing you should do is convey that knowledge honestly and without thought to keyword optimization. The problem starts, however, when all your deep knowledge is conveyed on web pages within the linked pages of your website. This often means that your index page does not get the search engine response that it should, because none of the pertinent "expert knowledge" is on that page – you have to click on links to get to it. This is when the mini-site idea very often reacts with search engines better than the larger site, because essentially your main page is one long sales letter which will be chock full of keywords, quite naturally. You shouldn't have to place too many extra keywords, if any, to get the page to react. All that you will need to do is optimize the source code, and I will get to that a little later.

So, with this in mind, I would suggest you put your website together any way you want for now. If you choose to make the larger site (as opposed to the mini-site), by all means link to all the juicy detailed stuff from your index page and we will talk about adding appropriate text to your index page to help it react well in *Google*.

Remember the main reasons to have a website: **Get their e-mail address or get them to the order page!** Don't distract or confuse visitors. I love the idea of a website with a relatively small number of links on the main menu page. I like this because it limits the options. If someone is coming to my site, I don't really want them to wander off reading guest articles when they could be reading my sales letter and order my product. There is a fantastic way to do this: you implement one of those really annoying pop ups.

Pop ups

Popup pages have had a really bad rap and for the most part rightly so. They are generally abused and it's all a web surfer can do to close them out to get a little peace and quiet. Having said that, I have to tell you they work like magic. Out of, say, 12 people, 6 can't wait to close them, another 4 will read them then close them, and another 2 will actually click on a link from that popup page. That's a good conversion. The reason they work is because they come to YOU instead of you going to them. It is direct "in your face" advertising. Provided you prepare them correctly, and you invite a targeted demographic, there is every reason a visitor will pay attention. For instance, my **PlayJazzGuitar.com** website has a popup ad on the index page. When you get to that URL the popup says:

Become a PlayJazzGuitar.com member – It's Free!! Get free access to interviews/ articles/lessons/forums! Get a free jazz guitar lesson once a week for 18 weeks! Five amazing jazz guitarists reveal their tried and tested secrets!

Now, if you went to that website because you were interested in jazz guitar in the first place, why would you not be interested to find out more about that subject? It is targeted and is not that offensive. On the other hand, if you went to my jazz guitar site and there was a popup advertising "Generic

Viagra", I may receive some hate mail, and I would thoroughly deserve everything I got! More importantly, my popup link to an entirely different demographic will result in zero sales. Nobody wins.

Your popup should either be an opt in subscriber form or should link to a carefully prepared sales letter with testimonials about your targeted product, a money back guarantee and a click to buy button at the bottom. Without that popup, visitors will have to stumble on your sales letter through another link and they may not stay to find it. A popup tells them instantly where to go and increases your percentage of sales. You can copy and paste a popup code at this URL:

http://www.aandronline.com/wps/scripts/auto_pop_up.html

"product_popup.html" can be renamed as necessary. The height and width can also be changed as can the browser specifics. You will need to make the **product_popup.html** web page and save it in the same directory. Make sure that the link from your popup opens in a new window (target="_blank"), otherwise your sales letter page will be displayed within your little popup window space.

Timed popups are really cool too. When you set them to go off in 30 seconds or so, it can be effective. To copy and paste code for this script go here:

http://www.aandronline.com/wps/scripts/delayed_popup.html

Another extremely effective popup is the "popup on leave" script. A popup opens when a visitor closes out a web page. You can add a popup to say something like: *"Thanks for stopping by, please consider signing up for our monthly newsletter"* and so on. To view, copy & paste popup on leave code visit this URL:

http://www.aandronline.com/wps/scripts/popup_on_leave.html

Before you go programming your popups, I have some extremely important information to tell you. There is a major problem with popups now. More and more people close them out without reading them, assuming they are spam, and of course many of them are. Almost everyone has a popup blocker now, so, although some of the above techniques can work, I STRONGLY recommend you implement the use of 'Hover Ads' instead.

The **Hover Ad** is a *layer* which means it is not a web page that one page links to. In other words, the Hover ad is part of the same page; it just appears as though it is a pop up. It floats down and asks if you want to opt in, and you can still close it out. The great thing about this script is that no pop up blocker can block it, or for now at least, because there is no pop up to block. Personally, as soon as I implemented this Hover Ad, my subscriber rate tripled. Needless to say, I highly recommend the Hover Ad. For more info visit:

http://www.marketingtips.com/hoverad

Keep 'em coming back

Not only is it important to get unique visitors for the first time but it is even more important to keep them returning. Why? Because as an expert you need to gain trust and respect from your visitors in order to get them to buy from you, and, just as importantly, buy again and again. There are several ways to do this: firstly, you add new content on a regular basis. This is a surefire way to get repeat traffic. The best way to notify folks when you have new stuff added to the site is through a subscriber based newsletter. Let's talk about that because this is imperative to a successful site.

Newsletter & subscribe box

On every page throughout your site you could have a subscribe box where visitors enter their name and e-mail address. This subscribe box will submit information to you so you can add contacts to your database. Once every two weeks you might send out a newsletter telling your subscribers about your site updates, up to the minute news and so on.

Below is an example of how you might display your subscribe box. In order to get the information to be sent somewhere, you will need a cgi script. Matt Wright has the most popular one called *FormMail*. You can download a free one at: **http://www.scriptarchive.com**. You should configure this script to work on your server and place it in your cgi-bin.

```
                                                            [Close]
* Subscribe to our free newsletter
"The Inside Scoop"
Get music marketing tips, record deal shopping advice
and exclusive 'must-read' articles every two weeks.

* Bonus! Get our FREE A&R Online indie artist
"Wake Up E-Course!"
Put your artist career on the map this week with this our 7 day
intensive music promo course.


          Email   [                    ]

     First Name   [                    ]

     Last Name    [                    ]


                  [    Subscribe    ]
```

You will need to insert a <form></form> tag in your web page which should look something like this:

<form action="http://www.yoursite.com/cgi-bin/FormMail.cgi" method="post">

You will also need to add some "hidden fields" like this:

<input type="hidden" name="required" value="e-mail,realname">
<input type="hidden" name="redirect" value="http://www.yoursite.com/thanks.html">
<input type="hidden" name="recipient" value="e-mail@yoursite.com">
<input type="hidden" name="subject" value="Another newsletter subscriber">

You can copy and paste this code at:
http://www.aandronline.com/wps/scripts/form_hidden_fields.html

When you purchase space from a web host, the company should be able to configure your cgi script so it will work on your website. Sometimes they do not, so it might take a call into tech support, but there is no excuse for a web host not supporting a cgi-bin and configuring it for you.

Your regular newsletter is one of the most powerful mediums you have on your website to make sales online. Remember when I said your website should have two main goals: *sell products and collect e-mail addresses?* Well, whenever you collect e-mail addresses from opt-in subscribers, you have the licence to e-mail them personally and seduce them further into selling your products. You could:

1) Send out a free regular newsletter telling subscribers what is new on your website.

This is the most common. You mail out an e-blast to subscribers with a list of links and brief descriptions about new stuff on your website. You might also take advantage of advertising your own product, any affiliate products you are currently selling or any paid advertising from third parties. (Paid advertising is only really feasible once your subscriber base reaches an opt-in target of say 10,000.)

2) Send out a free newsletter to subscribers with articles written by you or eminent pros in your field.

I like this one. Subscribers opt into a regular newsletter featuring articles written by experts. One of these experts should be you. You can easily find others who want to donate articles in exchange for a positive description and a nice fat link to their website. Traffic to their site as a result of an article donation is considered fair exchange.

3) Send out a paid subscription newsletter.

This can be extremely lucrative. If you offer expert knowledge, inside or exclusive information on a particular subject that has a value, you can and should send out a newsletter and charge a fee for it. There is nothing as wonderful as recurring billing and this is a great way to get it! If you charge say £10 a year for a newsletter and you have 10,000 subscribers, then your annual income from this newsletter alone would be £100,000. That is one hell of an income! And the best part of it is that you only have to write a newsletter every 2 weeks! Of course getting this many subscribers takes time but it's a numbers game I would be excited about, that's for sure.

Give something away free

There is nothing more powerful than the word "free" – or so the marketers have been telling us for years. This might have been true in the past but as far as I am concerned, things are very different now, at least online. People have abused the use of the word "free" so much so that now Internet surfers just don't believe it anymore. Let's take the adult website business model. (Big disclaimer: I am not a porn surfer – really I'm not!) Pretty much every single adult website will offer "free membership" or free admission" or "free XXX videos and nude photos". Now they even say *"I'm sure you are sick of promises of FREE admission, so boy have we got the deal for you!"* and so on. What they mean by "free" is this: Give us your name, e-mail address and credit card # and you can surf our XXX website absolutely free for 1 week and if you don't like it you can discontinue your membership at anytime". What an absolute CROCK!! There is nothing to me that spells FREE in any way shape or form here. Why? Because you probably have to jump through hoops to discontinue membership and of course they are relying on the fact that you will probably forget to discontinue, in which case you get a credit card statement with a transaction on it that will do nothing but piss you off! If I am going to get something free, why on earth do I have to give my credit card information to someone? It wreaks of slime to me. Now don't get me wrong, the adult industry is still the most profitable of all web businesses. I just think the template has been set to mistrust it. I wouldn't personally have anything to do with these sites, even though I might be partial to naked women displayed in all file formats! But that's just me.

So I suggest you actually DO give something away for free on your website, legitimately. Visitors will love it and probably return to your site often if the free gift was of value to them. When I say "free gift" I would suggest you give away a promotional eBook as it requires no work on your part once you set it up. The object as far as you are concerned is to turn a free gift into a way of seducing folks into your lair, you know, eventually to the credit card server. Rather than litter your eBook with banner ads for your products I would suggest you offer more of a mini "how-to" article with text links pointing to your products as well as any affiliate products you are selling. You could also give away a downloadable free video. This is stunning as it offers you the forum to speak about your products for sale.

Let's assume you have a website all about how to buy property to let. The main focus of your site is to sell your self-penned eBook *"Make A Fortune Tomorrow By Letting Property Today"* Your eBook sells for £17.99 and to many visitors it looks extremely appetizing where most buy straight from your sales letter page. But the odd cynic will need a little nurturing. They need stroking and a little more substance to get their teeth into something written by an author they have never heard of. And who can blame them? So you offer a free eBook with a very focused subject. Something like:

"Learn how to buy foreclosures in 7 days!" Now we all know that the property business is a wide topic, so why not give away a free eBook about just some of it. Inside the eBook you could talk about the subject in some kind of detail, and mention your big eBook on sale several times with links to the sales letter page. You could also link to some other affiliate products but your main focus should be to point them to the principal product you are selling. Now, since they subscribed, you also have their e-mail address, so what do you do with it? You add them to your free newsletter subscription and give them an easy way to unsubscribe when they receive it. Provided you offer something of value in your newsletter, you have many more attempts at selling your eBook. It's a numbers game.

eBooks

Now might be a good time to explain how to put together an eBook. It sounds like a whole big deal but frankly it takes about 10 seconds, once you have written the text! You need eBook software which is not that expensive. Once you write the book, you simply import the file (preferably an html file) and push "create eBook". It's that simple. Of course it will take a while to design the eBook in your html authoring software but once you learn how to make a website, it's exactly the same thing.

There is one small hitch though: as you know, there are two computer platforms; MAC & PC. For some bizarre reason they still haven't invented an html eBook platform that reads on both formats. When someone does, I guarantee they will make a small fortune.

.exe format

Right now we have the .exe (executable file) self extracting programme that PC users can utilize. This, to me, is the best format for eBooks, as it reads just like a website offline. The limitations are such that it is difficult to print all the pages at one time because, like a website, you click to the next page to read on. Therefore, if you want to print all the pages, you would have to print them individually. Many people don't like .exe files because of the risk of viruses attached. Personally, I have good virus protection on my computer and this is something I don't have to worry about. The executable programme is certainly my favourite eBook format.

eBook security

Many writers are extremely concerned about piracy, file sharing, and so on. The good folks at the *Internet Marketing Center* have come up with a breakthrough design for distribution of eBooks in a safe and secure way for PC users. The programme is called *eBook Pro* (**www.ebookpro.com**) and it enables you to zip up your html work into an eBook and upload it to your server. When a purchaser downloads it, they are prompted to input a username and password and register it. Now, you the owner/controller, have access to an administration panel where you designate how many times a buyer can register. In other words, let's say he or she has two computers and they want to install your eBook on both, you set their registration to "2". This means it is absolutely impossible for that person to file share because anyone who downloaded the eBook or received it in an e-mail would be prompted to register and they wouldn't be allowed to, even if they entered the same username and password. You can set all registrations to a default setting or change individual ones and so on. The really cool thing is that on the rare occasion that someone wants a refund, you can disable their eBook altogether, so in effect it has been returned. eBook Pro in my opinion is the most advanced security eBook publishing software presently on the market.

.pdf format

MAC computers need to read eBooks written in **.pdf** file format. Now, the great thing about this format is that both PC users *and* MAC users can read them. It is indeed cross platform, but it is not an html document anymore; it is a rendered adobe pdf file. The advantage of the pdf document is that it is (like *Microsoft Word*) one long document that you scroll down to read. This means that you can print the whole file with one click. However, navigating a pdf file is not quite as easy. Images and fonts don't look as sharp, but it does print very well.

So, what is the answer as far as formatting your eBook is concerned? My advice is to present both formats. PC users can download the .exe version (or **.ebk** version if you use *eBook Pro*) and MAC users (and PC users who like pdf format) can download the printable pdfs.

In order to make **.pdf** files, you will need *Adobe Acrobat*. (**www.adobe.com**). These files also prohibit pirating of text (you cannot view source, copy and paste) and you can also password protect your file.

When someone either purchases an eBook from you or signs up for a free eBook gift, there are two ways to transport the file to them. Firstly, you can set up an autoresponder (I'll discuss these a little later) with a link to download the file, or you can set up an autoresponder with an eBook attached. Also, and a little primitively, you can manually send an e-mail back with either a link to download or an an eBook attached. My advice is to set up an autoresponder, as the whole idea of **complete automation is the key to an enjoyable online business.** You do want to go off and play golf after all, don't you?

eBook covers

I'm sure you have seen many eBook sales ads on the Internet with an image much like this:

We all know that when you buy an eBook, it doesn't actually come in a package like this because we are purchasing downloadable information. Even though we are not selling a hard back book, it looks much more attractive to the visitor. It looks professional and can be a very powerful sales tool. There are a few programmes that enable you to make your own 3D covers very easily and they are, for the most part, extremely affordable. One I recommend highly is the Virtual Cover Creator. (**www.virtual-cover-creator.net**). This programme allows you to make covers for a variety of different e-products including electronic magazines, books, thin books, wide box and more. There are many other cover creator wizards on the market besides this one. Hunt around the net to see what works for you.

Community building

If you opt for the large-style website as opposed to mini-site sales letter, it is always a good idea to get people talking together, preferably within the walls of your domain (although people talking positively about you on external sites is fab too!) People love being part of a club or elite circle. If you can attract a forum network, then you have an audience to sell your products to. I like the idea of a "members only" area to help this along. There are a couple of different ways you can approach this.

1) A free members' area to subscribers who submit an e-mail address.
Subscribers get a username and password to access the members' zone. You might add a bulletin board where folks can discuss and network amongst themselves.

You can get a fab bulletin board with all the bells and whistles from **www.phpbb.com**. You can also get a free bulletin board quite often with your hosting programme. If your host does not offer this as a supplemental download, you can always hunt the Internet to get a free board. Configuring them, however, is quite often a nightmare. Aside from a discussion forum, it will be up to you to creatively add other things in the members' area that will be of interest to your subscribers.

At my Play Jazz Guitar site I have a free members' area with a forum, free articles, lessons and audio interviews (which are mainly a selection of links to external sites). Now because my site is free, this gives me licence to advertise my latest CD and home study jazz course on many of the member pages. I also have an autoresponder set up thanking visitors for subscribing and a reminder to check out my course. About seven days later, I have another timed autoresponder that reminds them about the course and to let them know I would like any constructive feedback about the website. Sometimes you have to take advantage of direct marketing. I try not to miss a trick, provided it is not too intrusive. Of course at any step of the way, I make it a breeze to unsubscribe. If you are going to offer a free member's subscription, the trade off should be the licence to advertise your wares.

2) A paid member's subscription
This is another extremely lucrative avenue. Your paid members' area HAS to offer something of great value to the subscriber in order for them to continue subscribing.

There must be something that is regularly updated for this to work in your members' zone or else your subscribers do not need to remain subscribers. I have been toying with a new idea at **www.aandronline.com**, my resource for independent artists. I thought I might offer a music industry tip sheet once a month that gives artists direct inside information about career opportunities. They would also get access to an online database of up to the minute contacts in the record industry. At no time would there be an e-mail address or phone number or A&R personnel that would be outdated. Clearly, downloaded software goes out of date, but this online database would be perfect as part of a member's subscription as it would be so current. It would have a very high perceived value and serious artists, I think, would pay the money. Now, the downside to this is that 1) I don't want to write the tip sheet and 2) I certainly have no intention of calling all the record companies every week to make sure their staff haven't all been fired! The upside is that I would go to outside sources to make this happen; for companies that have already done the work, I would cut them in and make a deal with them. Kind of like an affiliate programme. I might throw in a couple of bonus eBooks for members signing up and maybe one or two other incentives. The model works well I think.

Think along "perceived value" lines if you are going to offer a paid membership. If there is value, you will get members subscribing. If there is no value, you won't. It's as simple as that.

Password protection

There are two simple ways to password protect your website: the first way is to insert some generated code into your web page. Provided the user inserts the correct password, he or she will be taken to the desired location. *CoffeeCup* has a super-simple programme called the *CoffeeCup Password Wizard* (**www.coffeecup.com/password-wizard**) for around £15.00. You can also download the trial version. The downside to this programme is that once you are sent to the location, you can bookmark the web page for future use. It is not totally password protected, not hack proof (mind you – is anything?). However, for simple free member zones I think this works perfectly well. I use this on my personal music site. You can see how it looks at **www.chrisstandring.com/groovy_stuff.html**.

The second and much more professional and fool proof way to password protect is via a solution called **.htaccess**. This is 100% free and I am going to give you the code and tell you how to set it up right here. You will need to make two text files. The first file will be called **.htpasswd**. (.htpasswd is the file extension. It is not file.htaccess or somepage.htaccess, it is simply named .htaccess.) Within this file, you will have any usernames and passwords you decide upon. For example, they will look like this: (Ignore dotted lines – they are to show example only)

```
------------------------------------------
joe_blow:34MK5W3CpRmZo
------------------------------------------
```

In this case your username is: joe_blow
The password is: splendid

You will see that the password has been encrypted. This is very easy to do and there is a handy online tool to instantly encrypt your passwords called the *.htpasswd encryption tool*. You can find it at:
http://www.4webhelp.net/us/password.php.

Bookmark it for future use. The .htpasswd file needs to go in your root directory. Next, you are going to save another file in the directory that you want password protecting. This file will be called .htaccess and looks something like this: (Again, ignore lines)

```
----------------------------------------------------------
AuthUserFile /home/yoursite/.htpasswd
AuthType Basic
AuthName "Member Page"
<LIMIT GET POST>
require valid-user
</LIMIT>
----------------------------------------------------------
```

To copy and paste this code go to:
http://www.aandronline.com/wps/scripts/htaccess.html

And that is it. It is extremely simple to set up and very effective. Make sure you configure the AuthUserFile in the **.htaccess** file correctly. You can always ask your web host to correct this, if you don't know the correct path. Many web hosts offer this **.htaccess** password protection bundled with their hosting services and they give you a really easy way to implement it from a control panel, without needing to code it.

Page includes

Let's talk about what pages you should include within your site map. Whilst it is entirely up to you what pages you include in your site, I think, for the most part, visitors need to find certain pages with ease. The following links to pages on your site should be easily found on *every* page on your site:

- ## About Us

  Visitors to your site should be able to go to a web page and read a brief synopsis of your company and mission statement. If there are several individuals involved in your organization, then a small photo and resumé paragraph is appropriate.

- ## FAQ

  A frequently-asked-questions page is extremely helpful, especially if you are selling a subscription or series of products. This page will grow as more questions get asked but, in order to set up the page, you can no doubt assume a list of questions. It is usual to place all the questions at the top of the page with links to the answers below. You can do this by inserting a named anchor:

  `<a href="#faq1">Your question here</a>`

  and where your answer lies on the page, insert:

  `<a name="#faq1"></a>Your question here with answer`

- ## Member Login

  If you have a members' area, it should be easily accessible to subscribers. You can either have a login box or a simple text link which could call on your **.htaccess** password protect script.

- ## Contact

  If you don't have a contact e-mail or phone number, you will decrease your chances of sales! You must have this displayed easily on all pages within your site. Prompt responses from e-mailed questions always gets you in people's good books too. If you are worried about spam and spam bots stealing your e-mail address, then I have three solutions for you:

1) Make a small image in your paint programme with your e-mail address. Then you can link this to your mailto:joe@joeblow.com

2) Encrypt your e-mail address. Instead of the usual alphabet, you could encrypt all your vowels like this:
a = a e = e i = i o = o u = u

and finally:

3) Link to a contact form where visitors fill out their e-mail address and submit it to you.

- ## Testimonials
  The more folks you have talking you up, the more sales you will get. You should have a link to a testimonials page as well as a few example testimonials from your sales letter.

- ## Links (& link to us)
  When we come to discuss optimization, you will understand the necessity to have a links page, especially if you are a one man/woman organization that is relying on the web for as much free promotion as possible. Large corporations who spend huge amounts of money with sponsors and advertising tend NOT to have a links page. As a result their *Google* page rank goes up because (as of this writing) Google prefers websites that have more links pointing in (inbound) and less links pointing out (outbound). However, as the sole web meister, link trading will get you traffic and a perfectly good pagerank. Link popularity is everything – so go get it. Also, make it extremely easy for others to link back to you. More on this in detail later.

- ## Return Policy & Guarantee
  If you have a link to a web page that discusses your return policy and guarantee, you will instill good faith in potential customers. When you offer a lifetime guarantee or something like *"at any time if you are not satisfied we will refund you 100%"*, you create more sales. Also, provided your product is something of value and is legitimate, the amount of sales you will make will far outweigh your refunds.

- **Affiliates**

  Another extremely lucrative way to make money online is to offer an affiliate programme where your affiliates do the work for you. In return, you pay them well. I like to offer my affiliates 40% because I want them to have every incentive to work hard to get commissions. Make sure there is a link to your affiliate sign up page from every page on your website. This to be discussed in detail in a short while.

Audio files

Audio files have *huge* money making potential, which is the main reason I want to discuss them here. You can either stream an audio file or make it downloadable so users can play it from their computers offline. If you are selling original music online, the opportunity to stay ahead of the game and offer individual downloadable tracks is now key. Whilst many online music portals are still selling and shipping CDs, now might be a great time to think about selling individual tracks in order to burn from home computer systems. If users paid 50 pence per download, they could make up a compilation CD of their choice for just £5.00.

Another money making idea using audio might be to sell an audio coaching course, or expert "guru" style listener programme. If you have a good speaking voice, sound positive and upbeat, this might be a serious marketing consideration. You can sell the course online and set up an autoresponder with a link to either download the audio files or stream them on the web. (Alternatively, you can ship them a CD ROM if you like. Of course that is more work – aaaarrrgghh!!).

If you decide to keep your files online as downloads or streams, keep in mind that file sizes need to be fairly small for two reasons:

1) download time and
2) users need to be able to bookmark a file if they get distracted or have to stop the programme all of a sudden.

If you had one really long audio file, then finding where you left off might be a nightmare. If you have several files, then bookmarking will be a lot easier as users simply go to the last file they were listening to. OK so let's go into some detail with regard to setting up these files. There are several ways to add audio to your web page. I am going to talk about the three most popular:

- **Real Audio**
- **Mp3**
- **Flash**

Real Audio

This is possibly the oldest and most widespread format to hear music on the net. Most web hosting companies now have a licence to stream audio files so adopting the following principles shouldn't be an issue. Follow the steps below to find out how to stream a real audio file over the Internet.

Step one – extract the raw audio.

Firstly, you need to get the audio in its raw form into your computer. You have to extract the audio so you can make a .wav file. I like to use *Audiograbber*. (**www.audiograbber.com-us.net**) It is extremely user friendly and now available free of charge. You can download a trial version to see if you like it. There are many software programmes that do the same thing. However, I wouldn't advise getting a programme that rips music *and* makes the real audio file all in one programme, unless it is a real audio manufactured programme itself. The reason for this is that the real audio producer will produce the best, most optimal sounding real audio files.

Step two – make the real audio file

OK, so you have ripped your audio file and made a .wav file. You should now input this file into the real audio media programme. *Real Networks,* the company who makes these programmes, seem to update their software often. I have been using the *Real Audio Producer* for some time. (**www.realnetworks.com/products/producer/basic.html**) There is a free basic version which may well be all you need and a "Producer Plus" for around £120. Download the free basic version first and get a feel for how it works. It is simple enough to make the real audio file. You should hardly even need to follow instructions. Simply input the .wav file, click "encode" and it will automatically be saved as a **.rm** file in the same directory. Let's assume you have saved your real audio file as mysong.rm Now upload this file to the **audio folder** on your server. If you don't have an audio folder, then create one.

Step three – make a .ram file

Now you have to make a little text file with a line of code which will tell the real audio player to stream. It's very simple. Open a text editor, preferably notepad. In this file you will write out the absolute path to your real audio mysong.rm file. Something like this:

```
--------------------------------------------------------------
http://www.yoursite.com/audio/mysong.rm
--------------------------------------------------------------
```

That is all you should include in this file. Now save this in your **audio folder** as mysong.ram and upload it to your audio folder online.

Step four – make a link in your html web page

Finally, in your web page you will make a link to the **.ram** file (NOT the **.rm** file) The link on your web page will call the **.ram** file which in turn will command the real audio player on someone's computer to stream the file…. Ta-dah!!

One more thing: you may wish to edit your **.wav** files before you make your real audio files. For instance, you might wish to present just a sample of a song online and do a short version with a fade, or edit out some strange articulation in a class speech you want to present online. All edits should be done before you make the real audio file. You might check out a very comprehensive programme called *Sound Forge* (**www.sonymediasoftware.com/Products**). It ain't cheap (around 200 quid) but it is pretty amazing. It also allows you to make any type of audio file presently available on the web. You can download it for a 30 day trial. Now, if you want to spend just a few pennies and do simple .wav edits, you can purchase a wave editor from *FlexiMusic* (**www.fleximusic.com**) for about £8.00. Hunt around on the web for something that appeals. There are literally hundreds of editing programmes to choose from.

MP3

Mp3 files are all the rage these days and making them is a breeze. Like the real audio files, you need to extract the raw file (rip) and then process into an mp3 file. There are many programmes now that do all this in one and for the most part they all get the job done. *Sound Forge* is good but hellishly expensive, if it is just mp3s you are making. I would recommend *Audiograbber,* (**www.audiograbber.com-us.net**) a ripper and mp3 maker in one, now a free download. Can't say fairer than that! Just bear in mind that you can encode mp3 files at different bit rates which affects sound quality. Save your files around 196 kbps and they will sound damn near CD quality, certainly on a home computer system. Of course the larger the bit rate the larger the file and when you are uploading mp3s to your server, you want to save as much server space as possible. Save the mp3 file as something like: **mysong.mp3** and then upload it to your **audio folder** online. Then, from your html web page, you can link straight to the mp3 file.

Flash Audio

Flash (**www.flash.com**) is probably the fastest way to instantly stream an audio file on the web and the quality is excellent. If you have a music website where you want to stream audio instantly as soon as a visitor hits the page, this is the perfect file format. There is no time lapse and there is no music player programme that pops up and distracts you from reading. This can be a powerful direct marketing tool. Got a new single on the radio? Hit 'em in the eye with it! If you have a special news message for your visitors, you can *"Click here for news bulletin from our CEO"* and link straight to a popup window (perhaps with a photo of your boss) that streams an audio file. The Flash file will stream instantly and as soon as visitors have heard enough, they simply close out the window.

There is a fabulous tool I discovered called the *MP3 Stream Creator,* (**www.guangmingsoft.net/msc**) which takes an audio file such as **.mp3** or **.wav** and converts it to Flash audio. It will even give you a sexy play button with rewind and pause, and you don't have to learn the Flash programme in any way. It is also a batch converter so you can drag as many audio files as you want and it will convert them all in seconds. Highly recommended.

Video

Video is a growing medium on the world wide web and for live streaming, there are a few ways to go:

1) Quicktime

Quicktime is Apple Mac's default window player and will play **.mov** video format. PC Users can also play quicktime. The quality is competitive but I don't like a player popping up and intruding in the visual experience. Just a personal thing.

2) Windows Media

The *Windows Media Player* (**www.microsoft.com**) will play a number of formats including **.mp3**, **.avi** and **.wmv** but is only available to PC users (MAC users need to install extra software.) It is possible to embed this player into html so it appears seamless but I'm not a big fan because of the MAC issue.

3) Flash

My personal favourite because it is seamless and invisible to the end user. In other words, you can embed the video into your html and it will stream, and both MAC and PC users can view it. (All computers come loaded with the *Flash* plugin now.) Quality is absolutely fine. I have also found a really nifty video converter called *Flash Video Studio* (**www.flashvideostudio.com**) that will take my video, let's say in Windows Media Format, Mpeg or *Quicktime*, and convert it to Flash, AND automatically install attractive flash buttons such as play, pause, sound on or off etc, and give you the option to choose from a number of player designs. This is a must if you are streaming video on the web or offering video in an eBook or course programme. This would be a huge design job to do in the Flash programme so, again, this user friendly programme is hugely recommended for around £25.00.

Miscellaneous site additions

There are many bells and whistles you can add to your website but I think you need to be cautious of how much you do add. Simplicity is the key. Remember your focus is to get them to the order page in the smoothest way possible and too many groovy distractions will not help the cause. However, there are one or two things that you might think about adding to your site:

Search box

If you have a large site, then a search engine that spiders within the walls of your domain will help visitors find what they are looking for. If you have a website that has less than 500 pages, then you can get a free search engine from **www.atomz.com**, now known as *Web Side Story*. If you have more than 500 pages, you will have to pay. I use this search engine on all my sites and it is excellent. It enables you to place your logo on the search results and configure background and font colours so they sit with the design of your site. Also the really cool thing about this search engine is that it will give you an indexing report so you can see if your site is linked properly. For example: you have a site with 90 pages and you manually run an *Atomz* search engine index of your site and the report tells you that only 83 pages were indexed. The report will also display any pages with broken links. If you see that not all pages were indexed, it means that you can go back to your web design programme and repair your broken links. This is a fabulous way to learn about linking, as you can test manually as often as you like. Once you get it right with your local search engine, then you know that when *Google* comes a-hunting, everything's gonna be OK.

Another great search engine that you can configure to use on a CD ROM or website is the *Zoom Search Engine*. (**www.wrensoft.com/zoom**). If I was to go with a search engine online, I would probably recommend the Atomz product but for CD ROMs and eBooks, the Zoom engine is just fabulous because it is a javascript that works independently.

Drop Down Menus

I like these. They look like this:

You must understand that:

search engines *DO NOT* recognize this form of site linking!

A few years ago I made a website and I used a drop down menu to list my links from the index page. I ran an *Atomz* search index and the report told me that only one of my pages got indexed. I figured out that search engine spiders do not recognize the <option></option> tag. They only recognize <a href="webpage.html">text here </a>. I'm glad I figured that out before the big search engines crawled my site (or didn't as the case would have been). So if you are going to add a drop down, make sure that your web pages are linked from text links as well.

Tell a friend script

One way marketers suggest you get traffic is to add a button that prompts visitors to tell their friends about your website. Now I have to be honest and tell you I am somewhat cynical regarding how effective this actually is. I would hazard a guess to say that a tiny percentage of people really grab this button and use it. Of course I'm sure it does happen and it probably depends on what type of website we are talking about, but I can tell you I personally don't remember ever forwarding websites to friends of mine more than 2 or 3 times in my life. I very often forward e-mails but not website URLs. (Perhaps the curmudgeon once again?) Nevertheless, I am not one to balk at tried and tested theories so I would suggest you add one of these scripts if it excites you at all. If it does, you can add a simple script at www.aandronline.com/wps/scripts/email_2_friend.html.

Hit counter

This is something that will help you assess the effectiveness of your promotion on the Internet. I have a hit counter on my index page on all my sites. Whilst a hit counter on one page does not necessarily tell you how many absolute visitors you are getting daily (because many visitors can enter your site from other pages within your site) it will help you optimize your most important page – your home page.

It is important to know something about these counters and I find most web masters use the confusion to their advantage. A "hit" is very different from a "visit". A hit on a web page is defined as a file sent to a browser by a web server. For example, if you have a page with 10 pictures, then a request to a server to view that page generates 11 hits (10 for the pictures, and one for the html file). A page view can contain hundreds of hits. This is the reason that we need to measure page views and not hits. Hits are not a reliable way to measure website traffic. When a webmaster tells you he or she is getting 50,000 hits a day, then you can take it with a pinch of salt. You should probably reply with "Yes but how many unique visits are you getting?". I am convinced most webmasters completely make up the amount of traffic they are getting to their website in order to hype their perception level, if not to sell more expensive advertising. I know the real stats 'cos I am on page one of the search engine results in *Google* for ALL my sites and I can tell you I ain't getting 50,000 visits per day on ANY of them! Having said that, I don't have a Pamela Anderson shrine as of this writing. (Hmmmm...)

But I digress. Most web hosts will give you a web server log file analysis programme. It may be from *Webtrends* (**www.webtrends.com**) or *The Webalizer* (**www.webalizer.com**) or any number of different programmes. Most of them will give your page a good thorough analysis. I like *TheCounter.com* (**www.thecounter.com**) if I am going to use a counter at all. It reports very effectively. Gives you a daily visitor count, the last 30 referenced, (the URL that the visitor came from to go to your site), the last 10 search engine queries, which will tell you what keywords are successfully finding your website and much more. When you sign up, you get a very simple piece of code to add to your page and they will even e-mail you an activity report once a week. For about £12.00 a year, I think this is money well spent.

One final thought about hit counters: if you have to display a viewable counter at the bottom of your page, do yourself a favour and make sure you are getting an impressive amount of traffic first. It might be a little embarrassing if you are getting 10 visitors a day, at least for a while. I would always opt for the invisible counter. (*TheCounter.com* gives you this option). Actually I would go further; If I had my Pamela Anderson site and getting 50,000 unique visitors a day I would still not display a viewable counter (and let's face it who would be paying attention to it?). I just think counters look cumbersome and rarely are the colours and design complementary to your web page.

Free e-mail for your clients

Many websites offer free e-mail accounts to visitors. If you have a website called **www.splendid-trousers.com** for example, you could give away a free e-mail address such as **brian@splendid-trousers.com** and so on. The advantage to this is that it circulates your domain name. *Hotmail* did a very effective job giving away free accounts, and now everyone knows about Hotmail. Of course e-mail was their primary business model, but you could be like Hotmail on the side and have users login to your domain to get their e-mail. A bit of a job to set up but if you want to go the extra mile you can get more info at **www.everyone.net**.

Downloadable screensaver

Another relatively small but somewhat effective marketing device is to offer a free downloadable screensaver. You design an attractive screensaver with your logo, website address included and you simply give it away. I came across a fantastic one called the *Digital Photos Screensaver Maker* (www.photos-screensaver-maker.com) I love this and I found it to be a pretty good marketing tool. You make groovy slideshows by importing audio and images and send out really amazing, highly entertaining audio visual presentations. You can download an example at www.chrisstandring.com/movies/groovalicious.exe (A .exe programme for PC users only).

Javascripts

Javascripts are considered simple solutions for website designers. They are scripts that can be inserted into your html to dramatically enhance a user experience. Here are a few basic ones that you may need from time to time. Feel free to download all 19 in a zip file at: www.aandronline.com/wps/scripts/javascripts.zip.

Add bookmark	Link on submit
Auto popup	Popup on submit
Close window	Popup on click
Date	Popup on leave
Delayed popup	Popup once only
Disable right click	Preload images
E-mail to friend #1	Scrollbar colour change
E-mail to friend #2	Statusbar message scrolls
Framebuster	Title scroll
Highlight text	

Sales Letter

As far as selling products on your website is concerned, this will be your most important web page and one to spend as much time as necessary getting right. Whether you place a fat popup with a link to this page or whether this will actually be your index page itself, the page has to be set out so it grabs visitors' attention immediately.

As you know, there are millions of sales letter pitches online. Just do a search on "Internet marketing" or "get rich online", anything to attract a marketer's pitch. When you see a sales pitch, if it is a product that interests you, the chances are your emotions will be roused; it gets you kind of excited. And that is exactly what it is designed to do – get you to the credit card server! Buzz phrases like: "secrets untold", "discover how you can",

"Profit pulling power" and so on have a tremendous effect on people.

The key to a good sales letter is to focus on how the USER can benefit rather than explain how amazing your product is. Here's what I mean: look at the following two headings and ask yourself what would grab your interest most:

- *Discover How You Can Become A Wildly Successful Independent Recording Artist... Using Just A Handful Of These Little Known, But Amazing Strategies*
- *A&R Online, a highly respected organization, has been around since 1999 and offers tried and tested theories on how to get ahead in the music business*

The first sentence tells the reader how this product will positively affect his or her career. The second sentence tells the reader that the information is excellent because the company is firmly established. The problem with the second heading is that it's all about the company *selling* the product whilst the first sentence is all about the person *buying* the product. And that is the key to selling on the Internet, or anywhere for that matter. Visitors to your website subconsciously think "Who cares about the company? We want to know what's in it for us!"

So how do you go about getting a good sales letter? Well, you could study the fine art of writing sales letters yourself. I know I have stolen ideas from many sales letters I have seen on the Internet, changed things around and adopted them to work with my products, all to great effect. You could hire a professional sales letter copy writer who will tailor the best letter he or she can with regard to your specific product. (Expect to pay £££).

Finally, and my strongest suggestion, is that you purchase a sales letter wizard kit, essentially a database of templates that you configure to your own specific needs. You can spend hours, sometimes days manually writing a sales letter but you can achieve the same results in minutes using an instant sales letter kit. I would recommend Yanik Silver's *Instant Sales Letters* (**www.instantsalesletters.com**) Yanik's sale's pitch: *In Only $2^1/2$ Minutes You Can Quickly and Easily Create A Sales Letter Guaranteed To Sell Your Product Or Service...Without Writing!*

Your sales letter should have testimonials dotted throughout but you should not give the price of your product away until the very end. The whole idea is to seduce visitors first and get them really excited about what they are about to "discover". Oddly, it has been proven that long sales letters on the Internet work much better than short ones. I know, for me, if I am seriously interested in buying a product, I want to know a great deal about it. I want to feel sure that all my queries are covered, that previous buyers are ecstatic and so on. The more I know about the product, the chances are greater the seller will make a sale, at least from me. So, provided your letter continues to rouse the emotions and keep the visitor transfixed, a long sales letter will work beautifully.

Your return policy and guarantee should be outlined clearly, as people tend to purchase if they are comfortable that they have nothing to lose. Once in a while, you might get a cheapskate who wants a freebie, downloads an eBook, reads it and requests a refund. I'd like to believe that most people are honest and sincere, but there are always one or two. So, you know what, refund them and do it with a smile, because a) you have said you would and b) you will rarely need to refund if you have a bloody good product.

Towards the end of sales letters, marketers love to sweeten the pot by including a "bonus free gift for a limited time". This has become pretty standard now and works like a charm. People love "free" so make sure you throw in a little extra incentive. An eBook containing some pertinent articles works well. You could even have a collection of selected articles written by other experts, with their approval of course. You link to their sites from the eBook and everybody wins.

Your "Click To Buy" button can do one of two things: it can point them to your order page or it can go to another web page where you try to upsell another product for a "fabulous bargain". From what I have seen from my own sites, 50% of the time people buy the extra item when you do this. It works because readers are in a state of roused emotion from the sales letter and have at that point totally given in to purchasing, so to get them to buy one more thing actually isn't so hard to do. It's a psychological miracle!

PART THREE

Page Optimization

Search engine optimization

One of the reasons I decided to put this book together after so much time procrastinating is that I feel now that there are no real secrets anymore, just tried and tested ideas that few people are prepared to discuss. Sometime ago I felt like I knew stuff nobody else knew but then sometime later, it became apparent that many people who put in the same diligent hours figured it out too. So you may be asking why this course is different from any other. Well firstly, I don't believe there is one course out there that concentrates on all the pertinent details in one easy to understand document. I've read many many convoluted articles that haven't always measured up or haven't included important material that they should have. Secondly, even though others may know these secrets, few are divulging the way I am here. Search engine optimizers are extremely protective about what they know and they are hardly to blame for that. They are in an extremely lucrative business, after all. However, doing it the DIY way makes for hard work. The hours put in are so rewarding though, that you will be very glad you put them in. The really good news is that I have spent the last few years perfecting these strategies so you can take the advantageous position of making them work for you instantly. Let's have a look at how a search engine works in its simplest form.

Search engine crawling and indexing

A search engine spiders your website by following links from its point of entrance. It recognizes this:

<a href="webpage.html">text link here</a>

It reads the html of your web page. It does NOT see how beautifully designed your page may be, the way a visitor will view it. It has no interest in aesthetics because it is programmed to find pages that are linked from one page. So consequently you could have a horribly simple, poorly designed page with unattractive fonts and get to the top of the search engines, if the page obeys all the rules. This is very often the case, actually, and a bone of contention with many webmasters. Now, this is why it is so important to study the art of linking and, trust me, it is an art! If you are not properly linked, it means two things:

1) your website cannot be found.
2) all your hard work is in vain!

A website that is incorrectly linked is like a tree falling in the forest. It could be the most beautiful tree in the world but nobody will know or care. Now, there are two types of linking: a) internal and b) external.

> **Your internal links (links to pages within your domain)**
> **should be all connected together so a spider can get**
> **anywhere from any point WHEREVER it starts from!**

Your external links (links from other websites pointing to you and your reciprocal links pointing out to them) should also be set up correctly. Don't worry, we are going to get into all this in detail.

Search engine myths dispelled

You have probably been inundated over the years with invitations from search engine "experts" who tell you, for a one time fee of £££, they will submit your website to 6,000 search engines. Man, these guys have a nerve. Well I'm going to tell you right now that firstly there are not 6000 search engines (there are about 11 – all the others use the big ones to pull results from) secondly, providing you are power linked, you should NEVER EVER HAVE TO SUBMIT YOUR WEBSITE TO ANY SEARCH ENGINE!! The reason is that when you exchange links with (relevant) powerful websites (sites with a page rank of 4 and up), a search engine will spider those pages that have your link on it, follow that link to your web page and, with time, index your site. Now, if you are linked to let's say 4 powerful domains, I guarantee that your site will be indexed and will appear in *Google* search results within a month or two. You will need to make sure that the external web page that links to you is indexed by Google, otherwise it's a waste of time and you should not link to it. You do this by checking the site's *Google page rank*. (**http://toolbar.google.com**)

Let's say **www.nuts-and-bolts.com** links to you from their links page. Go to their domain, check the page rank of their index page and look for a text link to their partner links page. There should be a text link that says *"Resources"* or *"Partner links"* or *"Sites we like"* or just simply *"Links"*. If the partner links page is clearly connected from their index page, then you should be in good shape. It is then one simple step for *Google* to find you. I personally don't waste my time submitting to search engines anymore. I let them come to me. I feed them all they need and they come a-hunting. If you absolutely must submit your site manually, I suggest you only submit your index page to the big engines that allow you to submit without a submission fee. Their engine will spider the rest of your site, provided your internal links are set up properly.

Now, having made such a bold statement about never having to submit to search engines, I ought to tell you that there is a directory you *should* manually submit to and that is the *Open Directory.* (**www.dmoz.org**) It is not a search engine. The Open Directory Project (**www.dmoz.org**), in their own words, is *the largest, most comprehensive human-edited directory of the web.* It is constructed and maintained by a vast, global community of volunteer editors. The Open Directory uses volunteer editors to catalogue the web. Formerly known as NewHoo, it was launched in June 1998. It was acquired by *AOL Time Warner* in November 1998, and the company pledged that anyone would be able to use information from the directory through an open licence arrangement. The Open Directory is probably the only one you need to manually submit to because it's human powered and it won't come to you. You need to go and tell them you exist. The Open Directory provides additional search results for *AOL, Direct Hit, Hotbot, Google, Lycos* & *Netscape.* Make sure you submit your website to one category only.

Get Googling

We have talked about the big search engine *Google* (**www.google.com**). Google is so successful because it does not give extra weight to those companies who pay for placement (except Google Ad words – those sponsored results to the right of the page). This way, people who search know they are getting the best quality results. If you had a web page all about car racing and you bought a keyword "horse racing" and you came up high in the search results when someone typed in "horse racing", then that wouldn't be considered a quality result, (not to mention a complete waste of money). Google keeps its URL submission free so it can avoid this nonsense. All other search engines are now trying to adopt Google's principles to some extent so they can enjoy the same success. Many, of course, can't compete so their business model is usually a little different.

This is probably why many are going to a "pay for inclusion" model.

With this in mind, it might be a good idea to optimize your website for *Google* alone, as they are way way ahead of all others in popularity. They are so popular that many big web portals are using them to draw their own search results from. But mostly I like Google because I find what I am looking for. From time to time I might go to another search engine to see how it performs. I went to a big search engine recently, typed in "Jazz Guitar" and on page two found a website all about Britney Spears! All very nice but not relevant to my search.

Google and other search engines

Yahoo (www.yahoo.com) is still the most popular directory. It is important to understand that Yahoo is not a global search engine. It is screened by humans and extremely difficult, if not damn near impossible to get your website included. They don't like affiliates and they don't like marketers. They charge a whopping fee (last time I checked around £175) to assess your website. Yikes!! They don't even guarantee placement for that. Now, if they don't like affiliates or marketers, then I would hazard a guess that my £175 is money unwisely spent. Certainly for you and me. My advice is to avoid Yahoo's submission fee, as you don't necessarily need them, unless you are promoting a nonprofit site dedicated to the bushmen of the Kalahari desert, or similar informative resources. Yahoo, until February 2004, used *Google* for all their **web page results** (these are different from Yahoo's **website results** which come from their own directory), but now they have their own independent web crawler. Getting indexed in Yahoo is a very helpful thing and I believe, if you optimize your site and power link it the way I am going to show you, there is every chance you will show up in their results without having to pay exorbitant annual fees. OK Let's look at some other big search engines.

- *AOL* (www.aol.com) now has over 30 million subscribers and is therefore important. AOL search pulls all its results from *Google*. No need to submit to AOL if you are indexed with Google.

- *Netscape* (www.netscape.com) pulls search results from *The Open Directory, Overture, Google* and *RealNames*.

- *All The Web* (Fast) (**www.alltheweb.com**) boasts the largest engine and supplies search results to *Lycos*.

- *Hotbot* (**www.hotbot.com**) receives results from *The Open Directory*, *Direct Hit* and *Inktomi*.

- *Lycos* (**www.lycos.com**) pulls from *All The Web, Direct Hit, The Open Directory*. A paid submission programme.

- *Excite* (**www.excite.com**) pulls from *All The Web, Ask Jeeves, Inktomi, About, Looksmart, Find What* and *Overture*. There is now a paid submission fee to be included.

- *Looksmart* (**www.looksmart.com**) Also a paid submission to be included.

- *MSN* (**www.msn.com**) pulls from *Looksmart, Inktomi, Direct Hit, Real Names* and takes paid submissions through *Looksmart*.

- *Ask Jeeves* (**www.ask.com**) pulls from *Direct Hit* and others. It uses human editors and URL submission is free via e-mail.

- *Inktomi* (**http://submitit.bcentral.com/msnsubmit.htm**) is a huge search engine and provides results for *AOL, MSN, Iwon, Hotbot, Looksmart, Overture, NBCI* and others. No manual submission method.

You will notice that *Google* provides results for *AOL.com* and *Netscape*. That's 4 huge search engines in one! The above search engines are all valid, but small potatoes compared to Google right now. Because of Google's strength, I am going to talk from here on about optimizing specifically for Google. *"Is it wise to put all your eggs in one basket?"* you may well ask. The clear cut answer right now is YES! If things change anytime soon,then your mission is to deal with that as and when it arises but as of now, we are living in a Google world. (When things change, this handbook will be updated to reflect those changes). By optimizing your page for Google and implementing a carefully structured reciprocal link directory, the other search engines will also respond well.

Your link partners will provide a ton of direct traffic AND will add ranking fuel to all the other search engines!

I don't like paid search engine inclusion, especially if these other little engines are not giving me any traffic. Other than *Google,* there is one option which you should consider seriously to get high rankings and that is Pay-For-Click inclusion.

Pay 4 Click search engine inclusion

Pay-per-click inclusion enables people to pay a search engine to get their results high in the search engines instead of blindly hoping or by doing any real substantial work. Let's say you want to target the keyword: *"Guitar Amplifiers".* That keyword will have a highest bid, a bid which will enable #1 ranking. Now let's say the highest bid is 35 pence. If you want to get your web page all the way to the top of the results, you would have to bid 36 pence. This means that every time someone clicks on your link from a search results page, your account is debited 36 pence. Yes it can get pricey and sometimes companies tend to keep outbidding each other. When this happens, things get out of hand and it is not cost effective. At the end of the day REAL results mean sales from your website so you will have to measure up whether the cost per click makes sense regarding your sales conversion. One suggestion is to outbid the second or third ranking for that keyword which may be considerably cheaper and still get you on the first page of results. I think if you can get in the top 7 results from page one, you are still in good shape and things may make sense financially. I rarely click on the first URL I see from page one, I'll scan through a few titles to see which one grabs me the most.

Some keyword bids are just out of control. When my travel site, www.hotelchain.net was flourishing, it primarily targeted hotels in Las Vegas. At the time of this writing, the top bid for "Las Vegas Hotels" is around £2.00. By the time you read this, it will probably have changed. Now, understand that a normal web sales conversion is around 1%. This means that out of 100 visitors to your site, one of them will actually buy from you. If I bought this keyword today it would cost me £150.00 before I sold one hotel room. As an affiliate, this makes no sense to me whatsoever. So, should I decide to resurrect my travel site, it ain't gonna get results from pay per click! Looks like the tried and true old school method will have to suffice. Remember, I also have www.playjazzguitar.com where I target "jazz guitar" as one of my main keywords. Right now this goes for about 10 pence per click. Much more cost effective. Some time ago, I bought this and after a while realized I had no use for it because I was so high up in *Google* anyway from traditional "free" promotion (linking & page optimization), so it was wasted money every month. However, you should weigh up if this works for you. There are four online companies that offer this pay per click model:

Overture (www.content.overture.com/d)

Overture is the leading company for pay-per-click. The big advantage to buying keywords from Overture is that they display your results in *Alltheweb, AltaVista, Yahoo, MSN,* and many other portals, search engines, and web sites. This can certainly help in the early days of promoting your website. Yahoo purchased Overture in 2003 along with AltaVista, AllTheWeb, and *Inktomi* to own their own end to end search product. Also look into:

Google (www.google.com/adsense)

Google has a very popular pay-per-click program called *"AdSense"* which is similar to *Overture's* but targeted of course specifically to Google's search results.

Find What (www.findwhat.com)

Kanoodle (www.kanoodle.com)

Kanoodle and *Findwhat* are companies somewhat cheaper than *Overture* and *Google.* Now from my own experience, I get so little traffic from any search engine other than Google, *AOL* and *Yahoo* that I can hardly be bothered with them. Google is king. And I am absolutely in no way affiliated with them. Wish I was, bloody hell.

The search engine popularity contest right now goes something like this: (This chart is by no means absolute as things fluctuate daily – take as a mere approximation only).

Google.com	████████████████████████	68%
Yahoo.com	████████	22%
AOL.com	▉	3%
MSN	▉	2%
Altavista.com	▏	1%
Netscape.com	▏	1%
Askjeeves.com	▏	1%
Excite.com	▏	1%
Hotbot.com	▏	1%
Iwon.com		-
Teoma.com		-
Alltheweb.com		-

Spider food

Google uses four main principles to return its results:

- Domain name
- Meta information
- Body text
- Link popularity

If your website has all four of the above optimized properly, you should score very high in the search engines. If you get on page one of the results, you are in great shape. If you get on page two, you are still doing pretty good. If you get on page three, you will get some traffic and page four, well, not so great. But you can climb the ranks with time. So let's make sure we get up in the ranks as effectively as possible. Stay with me, 'cos I'm going to explain it all in black and white....

Getting a *feel* for good page optimization

There are one or two programmes you can get to help with page optimization and they are very good. However, I personally don't use them and never have. I now have a "feel" for what will work well and my hunches are usually correct. These programmes are guessing what will work well. They are educated programmed guesses and they are somewhat valid.

For the most part, I think you will do better with trial and error so you learn to get a gut feeling. One programme that is extremely reputable is the award winning *Web Position Gold* (**www.webposition.com**). Feel free to check it out, it might work for you. OK let's get to it....

Meta tags and hidden code

This is an extremely important part of optimizing your web page, so I will go into this in some detail. Meta tags are essentially hidden lines of code that reside in the html of your web page. This coding has a dramatic effect on how your web page responds in a search online. Here are the most important Meta tags to consider right now. You will see title, description and keywords. I have taken an example of Stock Car Racing to illustrate:

```
<head>
<title>Stock Car Racing</title>
<meta name="description" content="Stock car racing News regarding Nascar Winston Cup Busch Grand National and much more">
<meta name="keywords" content="Nascar, Winston Cup, Busch Grand National, Racing">
</head>
```

Notice that the meta content lies in the <head></head> part of the web page, essentially the first thing you see if you were to view the source code. (To view the source code of a web page, simply place your mouse over page text, right click and click on "view source". Your text editor, usually notepad, will display the code).

Now might be a good time to mention that **when a search engine crawls a web page, it crawls from top to bottom.** Therefore, if you have targeted a keyword such as "Stock Car Racing", a good idea would be to have that somewhere in your title.

Title

<title>Title goes here</title>

The title in your source code is *the most important line of text to optimize!*

If your website is **www.stock-car-racing.com** or some variation thereof, you might want to target the keyword phrase "Stock Car Racing". It's amazing to me how many web designers enter something like:

<title>Home Page</title>

or maybe

<title>Your complete guide to everything that has to do with racing cars – great service and discounts</title>

I even saw this one:

<title>Racing secrets – tips you won't find anywhere else</title>

Text that goes in your title tag should serve two purposes:

1) search engines will be able to index you well,
2) when your page shows up in the search results, the sentence reads well, is eye catching and makes the reader click on your link.

Point two is extremely important. There is nothing more annoying than seeing a line of keywords in a title in order to get a good ranking. Remember, it is about ranking but it is also about substance. With a little effort and creativity, you can accomplish both very well.

Title sentences should not be very long. Ideally no more than ten words. Don't forget that when your results show up, *Google* will only display approx. 60 characters. That is around 8 long words and 10 short ones. Keep this in mind, as longer titles will be cut off and your complete sentence won't be read. Keep it brief and to the point. I have found that successful title sentences usually begin with your main targeted keyword. For instance, let's target our "Stock Car Racing" keyword in our title once again.

On the next page are ten examples of good and not so good titles.

Title Example	Remarks
1) <title>Stock Car Racing</title>	Excellent. Google knows exactly what your web page is all about. Provided your website IS all about stock car racing, you are in good shape.
2) <title>Stock Car Racing – a complete guide</title>	This is still good. The second half of the sentence will read well in the results but won't help a keyword search, as nobody will be doing a search on "complete guide"
3) <title>A complete guide to Stock Car Racing</title>	It's difficult to say whether this would react well. It may well. Keywords appearing as the first and second word you read (aligned left) tend to react better than appearing later in a sentence, but there is no real way of proving this. Description and body text might be the deciding factor.
4) <title>Nascar Stock Car Racing</title>	Personally, this might react the best of all. I have had much success with my main keyword appearing as the second word in the sentence. A secondary keyword "Nascar" is also given weight.
5) <title>Everything Stock Car Racing</title>	Again, very good
6) <title>All your racing needs</title>	Not good
7) <title>News Directory: Magazines: Auto Racing</title>	Not good, unless you are targeting the keyword "auto racing" and even then I would stay away from the other words which aren't helping readers or search engines
8) <title>Motorspeedway news and reviews</title>	Not good
9) <title>Race cars</title>	Not good unless targeting "race cars"
10) <title>Cars</title>	Keyword too broad. Not good, as you are probably targeting a whole different demographic; probably those who want to buy or sell new and used cars, in which case you will be buried in the search results as your website is clearly about stock car racing.

I think you should effectively optimize your Meta tags with two or three *really* strong keywords. In your title, I think it is best to target your two main keywords. You can always get a third and maybe fourth keyword in your description and a few variations in your page body text. This is probably why I would go with example title #4.

Let's now take a look at a different subject and go over some examples. In this example you are promoting a company that sells greeting cards online. You are selling physical cards that can be purchased through your shopping cart sent via regular mail, as well as electronic greeting cards. Let's call your company **www.fabgreetingcards.com** or similar. You know the drill now.

	Title Example	Remarks
1)	`<title>Fab Greeting Cards</title>`	Very good, but you can target a few more keywords with this subject so I would want to include them somehow.
2)	`<title>Fab Greeting Cards – free printable electronic e-cards online</title>`	This is more like it
3)	`<title>Online Greeting Cards</title>`	Yes – great, but only one keyword targeted. ('Greeting cards' is considered one keyword, 'online' should not be a keyword to target)
4)	`<title>E Greeting Cards</title>`	Yup. Good but ditto.
5)	`<title>E-Cards by Fab Greeting Cards – printable birthday humourous anniversary virtual music</title>`	Might do very well but a bit spammy for me. Too many keywords without thought to sentence forming.
6)	`<title>Erotic greeting cards by Fab Greeting Cards</title>`	OK, if you are specializing in erotic cards. Don't like the word "greeting" repeated. No need to do this.
7)	`<title>Buy greeting cards online here</title>`	Reads well as a sentence but only one keyword targeted. That maybe OK but get a couple more in the description tag and body.
8)	`<title>Click here to buy online cards</title>`	Don't like this. Might get you buried.
9)	`<title>Cards online – all types</title>`	Don't like it. Not specific enough.

In the above example, I would go with example #2.

So you should probably have the <title> tag down by now. There is a lot of room for ideas, so play around until it feels right. Don't forget, you can always change it later. When you are seriously power linked, you can get *Google* to spider your page very often, as it will be finding your site from many external entrance points. I find, these days, that when I change my index page, I can expect Google to come crawling within 3 or 4 days. That gives me great opportunity to fine tune my pages. Okeydoke, let's talk about your description tag. It looks like this in your source code:

Description

<meta name="description" content="description here">

The description of your website is also extremely important to get right. It has less importance than the title tag but it is still extremely significant. Let's take a look at an example of a good description and title together. In this example, your company promotes baby gifts. Your website is something like **www.BeautifulBabyGifts.com** or similar.

	Title and description example	Remarks
1)	<title>Beautiful Baby Gifts</title> <META NAME="description" CONTENT="Personalized baby shower gift baskets and much more">	This is really good. Keywords you should target (according to Overture search term suggestion tool) are also "personalized", "baskets" and "shower". Keep in mind that as far as Google is concerned, the word "gift" is a separate keyword from "gifts". This is where your description tag comes in handy.
2)	<title>Baby Gifts, personalized baby shower gift baskets and more</title> <META NAME="description" CONTENT="Beautiful gifts for babies – stunning gift baskets for baby showers and special occasions">	Fabulous. You have all your keywords in the title tag so you can get creative with your description and make it read well.
3)	<title>Gifts for babies, baskets and presents for baby showers</title> <META NAME="description" CONTENT="Personalized baby gifts for babies and that special occasion">	Not quite as good, but might react well if your body page text is good. I would still go with example #2

Keywords

<meta name="keywords" content="place keywords here separated by commas">

Your meta keywords tag is, for the most part, of little importance. There was a time when all search engines looked at them, but now hardly any do. I think Inktomi is pretty much the only one now as far as I know. With that in mind, I suggest you add them anyway. Who knows? At some point things might turn around and all of a sudden the engines are using them! Simply just add your main keywords separated by commas like this:

<meta name="keywords" content="flowers, flower arranging, flowers delivered, flower delivery, buy flowers online, order flowers, mothers day">

Now you have a good solid template to work from. Make sure that every page on your web site has its own title and description. Don't simply copy and paste the same Meta info from your index page. This is important, because visitors can step through to your site from web pages other than your index page; something you can take advantage of. If *Google* returns pages within your site as well as your index page, you should not look this gift horse in the mouth. This is all well and good, as long as you include a good navigation system from *every* page within your site.

Meta tags and checking out your competition

Now what you might do is this: provided you have decided what your website is all about and you know exactly what product(s) you intend to sell on your site, you need to do a little research and check out your competition. Let's say you want to research your website that sells used laptop computers and the main keywords you are targeting are *"used laptop computers"* and perhaps *"used computers"*. Simply go to **Google.com**, type in your keyword and go to one of the first sites that comes up in the results. Right click your mouse and select "view source". The source code of that web page will then be displayed and you can examine the Meta info. Look at the title and description and keywords. Do this for 4 or 5 sites and get a feel for why Google is reacting well to them. **Don't simply steal another website's source code!** – make your web page your own! Once you feel like you have a good competitive edge on your Meta tags, you then have three more things to optimize: 1) body page 2) internal links 3) external links. OK let's go on with your page body text.

Optimizing the <Body> of your web page

Everything a visitor to your site sees will reside below the <body> tag in your source code. As I mentioned earlier, the most important web page you have to optimize is your index page. This is the page on your site that *Google* and all other search engines will prioritize. If you remember, I also mentioned that you should either have a sales letter on your index page or an introductory page outlining what your site is about. Here's something to think about:

If you use a sales letter as your main body of
text for your index page, you will need to do far
less keyword examination and repair work.

Why? Because *Google* has an uncanny way of distinguishing good substance over strategically keyword-placed text. If you write about your product, and you are an expert in your field, simply discussing your area of expertise in a flowing articulate way will inevitably put you in good standing. If you go for plan B – the brief introductory plan, then you will need to spend some time discussing your product to some extent so your body text gives enough weight to the spiders. As I mentioned earlier, there is nothing worse than a web page that has no substantial information for the user. The golden rule is this:

If your page has good user information,
then Google should react well too!

I'm not going to spend any time telling you how to optimize your page body text, because I want it to be **real** and not made up. Just write what you know. If you don't know anything about your website, then you may have a bigger problem than learning how to optimize it. My suggestion is to go and learn something about the subject at hand and offer not only useful information to users but information that users can't get on any other website. This will put you in the strongest position you can be. Once you have written your main body text, check that you have included a few of your main keywords you are targeting. Now, if the text is relevant, this shouldn't be an issue.

OK; so let's assume that you have written your sales letter or introductory text on your index page and you are very happy with it. There are a few more things to add to help get higher rankings. Let's call it "Spider food".

Heading tags

Any time you use a major heading, try to include one of your main keywords within it. Then add the following tag into your source code: <h1>**Your main heading with strong keyword placed here**</h1>. This tag tells the search engine that this is a very important heading and has a great deal of significance regarding the topic of your website. The theory is that if the search engine sees your Meta info and heading tags all containing strong keywords, it takes all the information into account when returning results.

Now you can separate your headings and sub headings using <h1> <h2> <h3> <h4> depending on keyword significance. The downside to using a heading tag is that it tends to give too much physical space below it. It seems to display the same space as a paragraph alignment <P> and there is no way to adjust it. (Look at the example below and you will see the space between the heading and the green table). With that in mind, this heading tag shouldn't be abused anyway so I suggest you use it sparingly. Remember when I mentioned that your web page gets spidered from top to bottom? Well I have had a great deal of success using a heading tag at the very top of my page, before any tables or columns. Like this:

Great Jazz Guitar Players: Wes Montgomery

The course | About author | FAQ | Order

Home | About Us | Courses | Testimonials | Return policy & guarantee | Affiliate programme | Links

After my Meta info, my heading tag <h1>**Great jazz guitar players: Wes Montgomery**</h1> is the first text in the body of my page that the search engine sees. Once it steps through to tables and columns, it has to wade through more code to find its keywords. If you start a page like this, you are in really great shape. The search engine pretty much now has all the info it needs and hasn't even got to your main body text yet!

Comment tags

The effective use of comment tags has recently been dispelled as myth. Webmasters used it as another way to add keywords to their html source code. A comment tag looks like this in the <head> of your html:

<!-- This page discusses these topics: Jazz Guitar, Jazz guitar lessons, how to play guitar, free guitar lessons, free jazz guitar lessons, home study jazz guitar course, play the guitar -->

Avoid the use of comment tags, as it is frankly not worth your while. Whilst it won't get you banned (unless you seriously abuse it), your time is better spent on other things.

Image ALT tags

These are very important and should not be overlooked. Back in the early days of cyberspace, there were primitive web browsers that could not display images. Sounds archaic now doesn't it? But nevertheless, those browsers did exist along with snail paced Internet speeds. Because images couldn't always be displayed, it was important, to some extent, to tell those browser users what they were missing. So an image ALT tag was included. It stands for *alternative text*. Even today, servers get clogged and, for whatever reason, cannot display an image, so it is still useful. It is also great search engine spider food because you can add a keyword or two in there. Like this:

This is what the properly displayed image might look like. On a computer you would mouse over to see the image ALT text.

Playjazzguitar.com

This image has either been corrupted or the server is down. If this is the case, the user will only see your ALT text.

Again, don't abuse this. The ideal is to get a strong keyword in there that also describes the image you don't see. Notice, I have chosen "jazz guitar lessons" which might be a good keyword to target. Keep your ALT text nice and small and don't write huge sentences; it's just too spammy, and spam is something the search engines can be programmed to find. If you get accused, then they can ban you and that is bad news baby, as getting un-banned is a bunch of hoola hoops you don't want to have to go through.

Text links versus image maps

Many web designers like to make images in a paint programme and divide that image up into links using an image mapper. Something like this:

Whilst I like image maps because they look cool, I rarely use them now.

Search engines CANNOT follow links to your other pages from image maps!

You should make sure that all your links pointing to different pages within your site come from text links. Text links that include keywords are also given strength by Google. If you absolutely have to use an image map, then make sure you also have a line of text with the same hyperlinks somewhere on your page, ideally at the very top but, provided your web page is not too long, then at the bottom will be fine. Something like this:

About Us | Contact Us | FAQ | Partner links

Index follow tag

Here's another tag you should include in your Meta:

<meta name="robots" content="index, follow">
<meta name="googlebot" content="index, follow">

The code simply tells the robot to index the page and to follow all links pointing from it. The second line is specific to *Google* and I like to include it always. If you *don't* want a search engine to spider a web page within your site, then add this code:

<meta name="robots" content="noindex, nofollow">
<meta name="googlebot" content="noindex, nofollow">

Naming files and folders correctly

Make sure your html **file names** have underscores separating words like this: **contact_us.html**.

Any **sub folder** in your directory should have a hyphen separating each word like this: partner-links/. Many beginners leave spaces in their folder names like this: partner links/. The consequence of this is that when a computer displays your folder name in the address bar of your browser, it automatically fills in the space with this: %20 Your folder name is then displayed thus: partner%20links/ I would avoid this at all costs. It's unattractive, unprofessional and you don't want any of your file names altered. Keep them nice and neat and follow the principles above, and you'll do just fine.

What to avoid at all costs

Let's go over the most important things to avoid when making your web pages. Some things we have briefly discussed, some we haven't.

- **Flash as your main index page**
  This will get you buried in the search results. Remember, *Google* and its followers cannot spider flash. The engines need static text to crawl.

- **Graphic overload**
  Too many graphics makes for slow loading web pages! Large graphics will

sometimes crash a computer. Keep graphics small or thumbnail links to full size photos opening in a new window.

- **Image maps**

  Avoid unless you add text links too (preferably with keyword within hyperlink).

- **Drop down "select" menus as site navigation**

  Drop down select lists are great, but search engines don't follow links using the <option></option> tag. If you need to use a drop down select list, make sure you have text links placed on your page as well.

- **Frames**

  Absolutely avoid at all costs, unless it is part of a zone in your website that does not require search engine indexing.

- **Dynamic page scripts**

  .asp .php or any database driven web page does not get indexed well on the web. Make sure your main index page is static **html**.

- **Symbols in URLs**

  Don't put any weird symbols in your file names. For safety, avoid spaces and use hyphen or underscore only.

- **Door way pages**

  This is an old trick that doesn't work anymore. These are individual web pages (often residing on external domains) optimized for certain keywords. This was a trend sometime ago when search engines were more equal in popularity. I think it is a bit spammy and a lot of work for generally nothing these days. The answer is good old fashioned substance on your index page and quality inbound links. Each page now has to have some link popularity to get good results, so if you are going to make a doorway page, you will need to link it successfully, in which case why bother? You might as well target your website pages.

- **Stealing code from high ranking sites**

  Doing this does not give you the same results as the page you are trying to outrank. I suggest sticking to your own really strong keywords (by all means research other sites and get good ideas; I strongly encourage it!). Build an overall strategy that includes coding and linking.

- ## Redirect scripts

    Sometimes referred to as refresh scripts, the meta refresh tag looks like this and should be avoided at all costs:

    <meta http-equiv="refresh" content="10;URL=http://www.yourname.com">

    This tag will redirect a web page immediately to another page. It is considered spam because many people would optimize a page and send it to the engines to target a keyword. When the results came up, users clicked on the URL and were instantly directed to another web page altogether. This will get you banned.

- ## Link Farms and free for all link pages

    Avoid at all costs. There are still many web companies that offer a link generating service. Essentially you get your URL on a list of links that everyone trades together. Search engines hate these and will ban you. You need targeted relevant links. Full stop.

- ## Spamming by e-mail and newsgroups

    The only way to get solid traffic is by hitting on a targeted demographic. The best way is by adopting pull techniques, not push. Getting high on search engines is the ultimate pull technique because visitors are seeking *you* out, not the other way around. Buying a list of 74 billion e-mail addresses is just nothing but trouble. When you send your e-blast, your ISP will probably shut you down and your conversion in sales won't be worth your while anyway. Placing spammy ads in newsgroup forums will have exactly the same effect. Don't waste your time!

    Rule of thumb: **Don't waste your time with short term illegal tricks**. You are dealing with computers, robots and experts that know more than you do. If you come up with an act of genius and it is illegal, then expect the engines to get hip to you pretty quick. You are building a legitimate business on the web. The ideas I am discussing in this course are highly effective and will enable longevity so you can continue to make £££. Do the work; you'll be really glad you did.

PART FOUR

Power Linking

Now you have your web pages optimized at least from a design and Meta standpoint, we should now go over in detail the fine art of linking. This is the most misunderstood aspect of website promotion.

Linking correctly will be the difference between some traffic to your website and PAGE ONE RANKINGS from search engine queries!

Firstly, let's talk about how you should link your website together internally. Stay with me really carefully, as I assure you this will be crucial to the success of your online business.

Internal linking

It is highly important that a search engine spider crawls every single one of your pages from any point of entrance within your domain. This means that if an engine arrives on your "contact us" web page, for example, it should easily be able to spider every single web page on your site from that page. The *Google* robot doesn't come around to your website every hour to spider your latest pages and, because sometimes it takes time to show up, it is important to set up your links correctly so it can manoeuvre through your site in the smoothest way. I'll give you an example of what I mean. Let's say you have a website consisting of just four pages and you link them together like this:

link ex 1

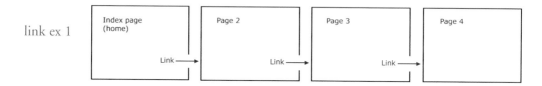

Notice that each link to each page is in series. The only way to get to page 4 is via page 3. I want to illustrate why you should not link like this. Let's assume *Google* comes a-spidering in January. Because you have a few external domains linking to your home page (**index.html**), Google manages to successfully cache that page and add it to its database. You have managed to get a good start. February comes along, Google comes back and manages to index page 2. March arrives and you get page 3 indexed. April falls by and page 4 doesn't get indexed. In fact page 4 doesn't get indexed for another 3 months. Turns out that your whole site of just four pages finally gets indexed by August 1st.

What went wrong? Why so long? The answer is simple. There are too many steps that the search engine has to take. What is more, none of the pages have back links, they all move forward to page four and stop. Let's see what happens when we link a little differently:

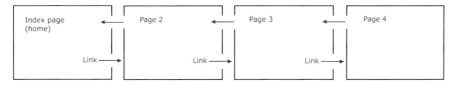

In the above example (link ex 2), you will notice there is a "back" link from each page. This is a little easier for a search engine to get to all the pages, but it is still flawed. If it arrives via page 4 (assuming there is an inbound link pointing to it), the search engine spider has a long way to travel to get to page 2. If it arrives from your index page (much more likely), it still has a long way to travel to get to page 4. The result? You might get all your pages indexed a little quicker but probably not. All you have really done is made it slightly easier to navigate from a user standpoint. OK, let's now discuss a third example:

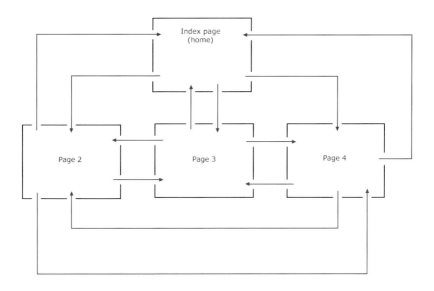

link ex 3

Link ex 3 shows all four pages linked perfectly. A search engine spider can crawl any four of the web pages from just one step. The result? *Google* comes spidering in January and indexes your home page. Come February all four pages are indexed immediately. Now this looks a little complicated to set up but in practice it is the simplest idea. Let's assume your four web pages are (for the sake of this demonstration) called:

- index.html
- page_2.html
- page_3.html
- page_4.html

You simply create the following links and **place it on every single one of your web pages:**

Home | Page 2 | Page 3 | Page 4

And that is the basis for structuring your linking internally. It's like a **mini link-ring.** Now your website, as it grows, may increase in size so dramatically that it might look ugly to add every single link on every single one of your pages. Also, a search engine might ban you for link farming, if the number of links gets out of control! Here is what I suggest (stay with me here as I'm going to get just a little deeper!)

For every sub folder you have i.e. www.yoursite.com/new-folder/, each web page within that sub folder should contain a mini link ring for that folder.

That way, each new folder has its own mini link ring. Now it's also important that, should a spider come a-crawling from any sub folder within your domain, that it can easily get to *every* web page within the rest of your domain. Here's a cool little trick: At the bottom of every web page throughout your website you are going to add a little copyright sign with text. Something like this:

© www.yoursite.com

This little line of text will link to a "site_map.html" web page. On that page, you are going to link to every page within your website. But let's not forget that search engines don't like link farms! Also, a visitor might land on that site map page somehow, especially if it turns up in a search results page so you need to make your site map page user friendly. Make sure that for every link to each web page there is a little description of what each page is about. Search engines like to see links along with descriptive text. (You could even put an internal search box at the top of your page so users can find what they are looking for). If your web site is not more than say 50 pages deep, this is not going to give you a great deal of work to do, but will optimize your site magically! The diagram below explains this concept a little more.

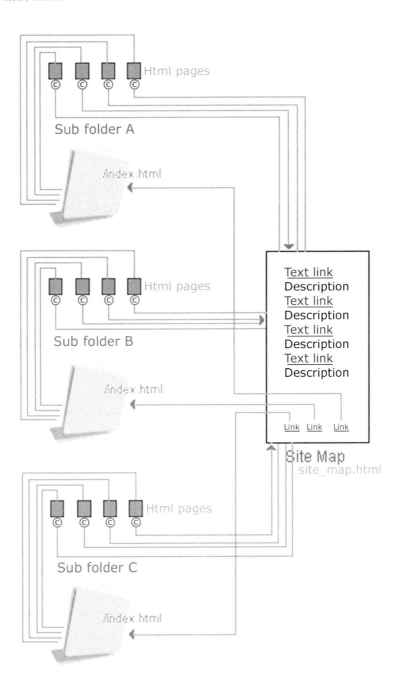

Notice each sub folder html page links out from the © (copyright text link) and links to the site map. The site map, in turn, links back to each individual html page within the sub folders. That way the search engines, wherever they land, can spider any page successfully within your site from any point of entrance.

If your website is large and gets larger by the week, you will have many sub folders with new pages added continually. In this case, you will need to add new links pointing to your new pages from your site map. If your site gets huge, you could even make mini site maps all pointing to each other from each sub folder. Just make sure *all* pages can be spidered from any one site map page and you will be in good shape.

So to illustrate this last example even further, (and I realize this maybe getting a little heavy) let's say you have a huge website with many sub folders and you decide to make a mini site map for each sub folder. You have 7 pages within a particular sub folder (i.e. www.yoursite.com/las-vegas-hotels/), you write links and descriptions to each of those 7 pages on your las-vegas-hotels mini site map. Let's also say that you have a total of 4 sub folders in your root directory. At the bottom of your las-vegas-hotels mini site map you add five more text links, four links to the index page of each sub folder and a link to your root directory index page (home). Now remember that keyword-heavy text links hold much more weight than just simple numbers or words so, taking this into consideration, one of your sub-folder mini-site map pages might look something like this:

Las Vegas Hotels

Aladdin
Aladdin bears the distinction of being the only resort in Las Vegas to rise from the dead, maintaining its original name and theme

Bally's Las Vegas Resort
Bally's is located in the heart of the Las Vegas Strip and offers its guests "A Touch of Class" with 2814 guest rooms and suites, 9 restaurants and celebrity entertainment.

Boardwalk Hotel & Casino
The Boardwalk's Coney Island facade and theme are popular among visitors to Las Vegas. So are the hotel's amenities and accommodation.

Caesars Palace Hotel & Casino

A world resplendent in regal pleasures...the zenith of impeccable service, and lavish accommodation.

Circus Circus Hotel Casino Las Vegas

Circus Circus invites you to come enjoy the Circus in Las Vegas. From nonstop gaming excitement, spacious rooms, and fine dining to entertainment, you'll find it all under the Big Top of Circus Circus.

Excalibur Hotel & Casino

Excalibur lives up to the grandeur of its surroundings with its breathtaking castle facade, overwhelming air, and flawlessly executed medieval theme.

Flamingo Las Vegas Hotel & Casino

The Flamingo Las Vegas is a self-contained casino and resort with everything to offer its guests — including 15 acres of a Caribbean-style water playground

Hotels in Europe | Book Rental Cars Online | Cheap flights | Taxi Cab Service | Home

Get the idea? The text links with title and descriptions point to the individual html pages within that sub folder and the text links at the bottom of the page point to the index pages of all the other sub folders including your home page.

And............ *rest.*

Let me tell you that this is a surefire way to get you indexed quickly and once you decide to adopt this internal linking strategy, you will be extremely glad you did. Remember, a search engine must be able to get to *any* of your web pages within one step. If you have a huge website that includes a database of static pages, then your search engine needs to be able to get to any of your pages within 2 steps.

Sub folders

A good general rule of thumb is to keep as many of your web pages in the root directory as possible. The reason for this is that the search engines have further to travel, the more sub folders you have. Sometimes you just have to have a sub folder to keep things organized but I would try to limit your sub folders as much as possible, as your pages will not rank as high the further away the crawlers have to travel from your root directory. Your site mapping will be easier to keep organized too.

Google and internal links

As we have discussed, the more links pointing to your domain the better. Now, if you are perfectly linked as I have just talked about, *Google* will love you for two reasons:

1)   Because the Googlebot will be able to crawl through your entire site with ease

Every page in your site will get indexed which means, providing you have optimized each individual page, visitors may stumble across your site from various points of entrance within your site (unless you instruct the robot otherwise). Because this can happen, you should advertise your products somehow on every web page.

2)   Internal links also carry weight which adds to your page rank

Contrary to much belief, *Google* **does** take internal links into account when measuring page rank. They are clearly not as valid as external inbound links but there is no question that a well linked domain (using anchor text) will be ranked a good deal higher than a poorly linked one.

OK. Can I suggest you go back and reread this section. It is heavy but *extremely* important. After you have got the idea and apply it once, it will be a piece of cake.

Test with local search engine

Remember a while ago I talked about implementing a search box on your website so visitors can search within your domain? I mentioned a free engine you can use called *Atomz*. If your site is under 500 pages, you can get this free of charge, along with a weekly search report in your e-mail. Once you have set up your web pages, interlinked using the above strategy, do a manual index of your entire website from your **Atomz.com** account online. After it has finished indexing, check that there are no errors or broken links. If there are, fix them. Now go to your search box on your website and run a few searches on certain keywords that you think visitors might use. Go to the results page and examine how your results come up. Do your web pages come up in the right order? Do the title and descriptions read well? Use this local search engine to fine tune your website pages. Once the results feel good to you, then you should be in good shape when the big boys come spidering.

External linking

OK. We have now come to the final step in page optimization. We have talked in detail about page layout, Meta info, body page text and internal linking. Now it's all about building a traffic flow towards your website. Remember, **your website is a tree falling in a forest with nobody around for miles**, if you don't get this last step right. There are two reasons we need to layout a reciprocal link strategy:

1) **So the search engines can rank your site really high**
2) **So you get traffic from other domains and you don't have to rely 100% on the search engines.**

Getting a good steady flow of traffic from search engines is a wonderful thing, but it is competitive and there are always other websites trying to outrank their competitors. If you were to trade links with many external sources, you would have a solid reliable stream of traffic in a way that you might not if you relied totally on search engines. Also, let's not forget that once in a while the search engines do change their algorithms so you may find your rankings go up and down somewhat. Trading links with the right sources will give you a good steady stream AND will fuel the search engines. Why? Because the engines now look at *link popularity* as a powerful contributing factor to the relevancy of a website. Link popularity is exactly what it says:

The more *quality* links pointing to your site the more powerful your ranking!

However, it is not just about trading with *any* site that will exchange a link with you. Some sites simply think it is a numbers game and the more the merrier. This is clearly not true. It is about quality links. Also a higher page rank is given to those sites that have more inbound links than outbound. This of course is hard to accomplish, especially if you are operating on a shoestring and using as much free promotion online as you can to get ahead. After all, why should a site link to you if you won't link back to them?

Now Google states that if the site that is linking to you is itself powerful (containing a good deal of inbound links), this will rank *your* site higher.

With this in mind, you should only trade links with sites that have a page rank equal or greater than yours. To get started, you may have to trade with a couple of sites with a low page rank (1/10 or 2/10) but, as you move upward, be a little more selective. Once again, ONLY link to sites that are relevant to your users. Set up a themed link directory, a new sub folder called resources. The path should be: www.yoursite.com/resources/ where you will have many categories that your links will reside under.

Let's assume you have a site all about success coaching; you know, personal goal setting, that kind of thing. You might have a link directory including the following categories:

• Authors (31)
• Personal Coaches (17)
• Neuro Linguistic Programming (5)
• Business Consulting (23)
• Health & Medicine (9)
• Financial Management (4)

And so on. The numbers in brackets tell the user how many links you have in that directory (optional). The way you set the directory up is similar to the way *Yahoo* or a major portal would, except that the subjects are only relevant to *your* visitors. Try to think of relevant themes. Imagine you are a web surfer and you are browsing through a website. What kind of website might you be reading through that would lead you to click on a link to go to your site? In the case of success coaching, it might be a site all about financial management or health. Ask yourself, *"Who wants success coaching, and where would those people hang out?"* Clearly, they would be at other success coaching sites and you should be linking to those, but it is also extremely smart to link to non-competitors' sites that might be relevant to your business. If you had a website all about wild dolphins, you might trade links with other sea mammal sites and so on. Put your thinking cap on. Conversely, if your website is all about *"Pets and how to care for them"*, you should avoid trading links with *"Travel sites or Stock Market Tips"*. Get the idea?

Build a solid flow of traffic, linking with solid relevant sites.

Make sure that each page of links has no more than 50 displayed. You can trade a small banner too but always make sure that if your reciprocal link partner displays your banner, they also display your keyword-laden (anchor text) hyperlink. Always go for a text link first because, as you have learned, the search engines need to spider static text. They can spider an image with a link (different from the way an image map is coded) but the keyword text link is actually what you need. A banner might catch a user's eye more, but as I say, that's all gravy.

You should display your links with a title (linked) and description like this:

Stanley's Stereo Systems
New and used car stereo systems, domestic and imported.

Cookie Callie's Car Alarms
High end alarm systems for all makes and models.

In the same way that your index page needs tons of links pointing towards it, ideally so do your links pages. Smart webmasters now look at the page rank of your links page more than they do the page rank of your home page. This is because the strength of the link pointing to their site from yours will be measured from *that* page and not your index page. It's all well and good having a high page rank on your home page but webmasters linking to you will get better results if your links page has a high page rank. I have devised a cool way to improve this and I am really surprised no one else has jumped on it sooner. If everyone took this as standard practice, all links pages would have a much higher page rank. It works like this: You display a link with title followed by description *and* a link to the page that your reciprocal link resides on. You could set it up like this:

Title	Description	Link back
Used cars for sale	Domestic and imported pre owned cars by George Smith & Co.	Link back
Car stereos and alarms	Car stereos and alarms for all makes and models by Chuck Seabiscuit.	Link back

This way, there is a link pointing to a partner links page, giving it extra search engine strength. Imagine if everyone did this? Giving weight to your partner's link page also gives weight to yours. Right now I see way too many link pages with no page rank because they are either not linked directly from their index page, or their links pages are too many sub folders away from their root directory.

As your site grows and your page rank increases, you will start to receive many link exchange proposals from external sites, many completely unrelated to yours and of course you should delete these immediately. Most of these unrelated link trade proposals are spammed using automated software. You should avoid any e-mail that looks like this, and there will be plenty. When you trade links, you need to outline some rules for other sites should they want to propose a trade with you. Something like this:

Important: this website will trade a link with webmasters who adhere to the following guidelines:
- Only relevant websites
- No dynamic script driven exchange pages – only static html please!
- Not more than 50 links per page.
- The exchange page should be linked directly from your main index page.
- Your website should have a Google page rank of at least 2
- The exchange page resides within your domain

Reciprocal link exchange software

"All this bloody work!" you might be thinking. Well just remember that a good link is like gold dust and every quality link you get will promote your business. There is, however, a fabulous tool to help you automate this somewhat tedious task. It is called *ARELIS* (**www.axandra.com**) and, I have to say, it actually makes link trading quite fun to do. I have been using this for sometime and it is fabulous because it searches the Internet for potential partners. You can go to your immediate competitor and ask Arelis

to return all the partners that link to *them,* the theory being that their partners should also be linking to you. You can also search the Internet by inputting a keyword. It makes finding new partners a breeze. Not only that, it will actually create your html link directory pages for you. You can update your link pages whenever you need to; you simply run a partner link check and it will tell you if your partners are still linking to you. All you need to do is upload your link pages to your server, which frankly is the easy bit anyway. It has built-in e-mail templates so you can communicate with your partners. You can simply propose a link trade or ask them why they have removed your link etc. etc.

All this is completely customizable of course. I would strongly recommend customizing, in fact you should write your own template from scratch. It is extremely annoying seeing link proposals where the sender has simply used a standard built in template. Make an effort at least! Here is an example e-mail proposal you might send:

<<recipient-first-name>>,

Would you like to exchange links with www.hotelchain.net, a very popular travel website? I have just placed a link to <<recipient-domain>>.

You can find the link to your site here: <<your-URL>>/<<recipient-sub-category-file-name>>

I've used this text to link to your site: "<<recipient-site-title>>"

This is the description I've used for your site: "<<recipient-links-page-link-description>>"

Let me know if you want to change the description of your site. Please add the following link info for HotelChain.net:

Title: Discount hotels in Las Vegas from HotelChain.net
URL: http://www.hotelchain.net
Description: "Book discount hotels, flights and rental cars worldwide"

Alternatively, simply copy and paste this code:

<a href="http://www.hotelchain.net" target="_blank" title="Hotels in Las Vegas">Discount hotels in Las Vegas from HotelChain.net</a>
"Book discount hotels, flights and rental cars worldwide"

Can you let me know where and when you link back? Thanks very much.
Sincerely,

Chris
www.hotelchain.net

Link exchange proposals via e-mail are completely standard now so don't be afraid to send them. It's a win-win situation for all concerned. Just make sure that when you are looking to exchange links that the site you request links with actually has a links page. Not only that, the links page is clearly visible from their index page. Occasionally a links page is not visible and if a user cannot get there easily, then what good is it to you?

I like *ARELIS* (**www.axandra.com**) because, although it automates much of the nightmare work, it still needs a human touch for it to work successfully. Clearly you need to be very selective regarding who you trade links with.

There are other automated reciprocal link programmes and I have looked into these. There are those 100% automated link programmes where you fill out a form and submit. The software then spiders the link you have placed pointing to their site and once it confirms the link, it immediately places a reciprocal link back to you. All this happens within seconds with no human intervention. The problem is, this solution invites all kinds of spamming. Any site can therefore link to you and it just doesn't do you any good. I have seen way too many of these pages with no page rank, which leads me to believe many of those pages get banned. Don't exchange links with sites that you think look a bit dodgy. I think you should be very precious about who you trade links with and avoid these software programmes like the plague. Stick with *ARELIS*, or *Zeus* (**www.cyber-robotics.com**) a similar program, or do it by hand.

Make it easy for others to link to you

It goes without saying that if a high page ranked site goes to your site looking to propose a link trade, you should make it easy for them to do so. I strongly recommend adding a custom link proposal contact form. The form is filled out, submitted to you and you get an e-mail with the exact info you need to trade a link. I have included an example contact form below which you are welcome to use and configure to your needs.

Link exchange program - Please set a link to us first! Click here for code

Contact Name

Email address

Title
(The name of your website IE: "Your Site.com ")

URL http://
(The web address IE: http://www.yourwebsite.com)

Description
(IE: "Patch quilts from southern Spain")

Google page rank 1/10
(Very important! select from drop down menu)

Your site has now placed a reciprocal link Yes

(Proposed) reciprocal link URL http://
(The EXACT URL that has the link back)

Comments

How did you hear about us?

Submit info

You can copy and paste this form code at:

http://www.aandronline.com/wps/scripts/link_proposal.html

If you don't add this to your site, you will be inundated with e-mails that don't include a description or reciprocal link URL etc. Frankly it can be chaotic. Use this contact form, I've done all the work for you.

Make sure they link to you properly

As I have mentioned a few times, a keyword-laden anchor text link goes a long way with the search engines. This theory holds for any links within your site or inbound links residing on external domains. However, a webmaster linking back to you often gets in the way of optimization.

Let's assume you have a website that sells cheap car insurance and your company is called Ray Clinkman Insurance LLC with a website at www.ray-clinkman.com. If you don't specify how your link should be displayed, the chances are your link will look like this:

Ray Clinkman Insurance

This is not the ideal. The optimal way to display your link would be like this:

<u>Cheap Car Insurance</u>
Quality affordable car insurance from Ray Clinkman Insurance LLC

The keyword "Cheap car insurance" is now the link text and the name of your company (which is inconsequential as far as optimizing is concerned) is now added to the description. There may also be some evidence to suggest that the title attribute can also add a slight ranking boost. Something like this:

```
<a href="http://www.ray-clinkman.com" title="Cheap car insurance">Cheap Car insurance</a>
```

You might consider offering webmasters html code to add a link to your site. This is a lot easier for webmasters on the whole as they simply have to copy and paste it into their link page. Your html code might look something like this:

```
<a href="http://www.ray-clinkman.com" title="Cheap car insurance">Cheap Car insurance</a>
<br>Quality affordable car insurance from Ray Clinkman Insurance LLC
```

One reason keyword heavy domain names do so well is because webmasters tend not to alter those titles. If the site is called **www.website-promotion-secrets.com**, then the chances are a webmaster won't change the title and you are guaranteed a good keyword-laden reciprocal text link.

Link trading etiquette

Trading links shouldn't be a pain in the neck but often can be. If webmasters all followed the same etiquette, it would be a lot smoother. Adhere to the following rules and you should be in good shape.

- **Put up a link before asking for a link**
  If you are going to propose a link trade to someone, then add their link first before you shoot off an e-mail. It shows you are serious, professional and will give the recipient an incentive to trade back.

- ## Make the link directory visible

  Very often a webmaster will add a link to his links directory and when you go there, your link is indeed visible. However, when you go to the home page there is no clear text link to that links directory. It's as if it is hidden. Too many webmasters are looking for high search engine rankings *only* so they try to hide their links directory. They create inbound links but hide the outbound links from search engines. Usually these hidden link directories will result in a zero page rank (although their home page may be ranked very high). Don't link to these sites. If a visitor cannot easily find your link, it is of absolutely no use to you.

- ## Add to relevant sites only

  Don't link to just anyone to get links. You will have more luck linking to 5 high page ranked sites than you would 50 irrelevant 1/10 ranked sites. Also, make sure that you are linking to external sites that are *also not* linking to every Tom Dick or Harry. A good way to measure this is to look at the links on the proposed partner site. If your site is about Italian cooking and you see links to sites selling Viagra products, member enlargement and mortgage refinancing, you know to steer clear of these guys!

- ## No more than 50 links per page

  We have talked about this. Keep your links page search engine friendly.

- ## Give exact URL

  When you propose a link trade, add your partner link first and, in your e-mail proposal, state the exact page that they can find their link on your site. I can't tell you how many times I get link requests from people saying they have added a link back to me and when I go to their directory I am hunting for 10 minutes trying to find it! Very often I can't find it because they haven't added it yet. When you propose a trade, don't simply give the URL of your links directory index page and say, *"You can find it in the appropriate category"*. No no no! Give them the *exact* path so they can get to it in one click. Time is precious.

- ## Don't spam for link requests

  Don't simply get a mailing list of websites and send a blanket e-mail requesting a link trade. If I don't see my personal e-mail address in the header of a link trade request, I know it has been spammed and they haven't even been to my site. I also know they haven't visited my site, because I have link proposal contact forms on all of them. If they had actually been there, they would have filled out my form. Spammed link requests don't go down well because they are usually from webmasters who are trying to cut corners at every possible turn. Send a personal e-mail to a site that you personally visit. (You can still use software like *ARELIS* or *Zeus* to help you find the sites and automate everything else).

- ## Keep your proposal short & sweet
  Long convoluted e-mails explaining "how trading links benefits everyone" really aren't necessary. Keep your e-mail short and to the point. Tell them where their link is, and exactly how they should link to you.

- ## Don't delete without good reason
  Once you add a link it should remain on a static html page unless there is good reason to delete it. If your partner has deleted his link, then by all means send an e-mail and give them an opportunity to repair it. If this is fruitless, then go ahead and delete.

Adding domains

Once you have some degree of success with one website, pretty soon you will want to start new sites for further cash profits, related or otherwise. Don't forget that you can take advantage of your additional domains to cross promote your other sites. You can add a little sub folder from each domain with links and descriptions to the other domain. You can also cross promote each site via your index page from each site.

PART FIVE

Making Money Online

E-Commerce

Once you set up your website, you will need to accept credit cards online. Accepting credit cards is an absolute must today, as you have to take advantage of the impulse buyer. This is what I like about selling downloadable information online. It is immediate, something that is appealing to a buyer. They can purchase using a credit card and, within minutes, receive the information they purchased. In order to accept credit cards, you will need a shopping cart, gateway and merchant account. Contrary to popular belief, setting this up is now a breeze, should you choose the right programme.

Shopping Cart & Gateway

The *1ShoppingCart.com* (**www.1shoppingcart.com**)programme is fast becoming the choice for all Internet entrepreneurs. It basically has everything bundled into one. It is extremely user friendly, very simple to set up and very affordable. The merchant account I use is *Authorize.Net* (**www.authorize.net**) which complements the 1ShoppingCart system perfectly. The two interact perfectly, as they have set it up that way.

The 1ShoppingCart system allows you to:

- Configure your shopping cart seamlessly into your website
- Implement an unlimited amount of timed autoresponders
- Manage your newsletter and broadcast (bulk e-mail) to your client list (html or text)
- Make money with its built-in affiliate programme
- Track your own ad campaigns using "Ad Tracker"
- Create custom web forms and popups
- View detailed sales reports, manage clients, search orders, "mark as refund" etc. etc.

1shoppingcart.com is a US based company, but the system allows you to set up your store using any currency you like. Because most Internet customers reside in the US, you might consider setting up your system using American dollars instead of British pounds. This, of course, is entirely up to you and very dependent on the product or service you are offering.

Other ways to collect money

The following payment methods should be offered *in addition* to credit cards and not instead of.

1) Paypal

Consider *PayPal* (**www.paypal.co.uk**). This is a very popular way to transfer funds over the Internet safely and securely. It is somewhat similar to taking credit cards but, effectively, buyers are sending money to your account online. They can even send money to your paypal account via your e-mail address. You can then withdraw money from your account; either you have a cheque cut and sent or have it credited directly to your bank account. I would advise that you give the option to purchase through PayPal in addition to taking all major credit cards. Paying with PayPal is still not as widely accepted as traditional credit cards, however.

2) Sending a cheque through regular mail

This is also an option that you should give your buyers. You set up a printable contact form that they send to you along with their cheque or money order. However, I must point out, if you are selling instant downloads there are a couple of disadvantages here:

- **The buyer has to wait until you receive the cheque to get his product**
  Not only is there a wait time but occasionally they will hand write an e-mail address that is illegible. This is painful, and not the kind of automation we have been trying to adopt!

- **Sometimes the cheque doesn't clear**
  You could wait for the cheque to clear, but then that gives you even more work to do. Monitoring cheque clearances is not the kind of fun we are trying to achieve! My advice is to trust that the cheque will clear and send them their product. Once in a great while you will get a dud. Not very often.

3) Cash delivered in a hollow tree at a specified date and time

This might be a little old school. Trust me, it's a lot easier to take credit cards! :)

103

Autoresponders

Autoresponders are a must if you want to make optimum sales from your website. When you create an autoresponder, you are essentially direct marketing, using permission from the subscriber. It works in a variety of ways:

ex #1 A visitor subscribes to your newsletter and they get an autoresponder saying "Thanks for subscribing" and a short paragraph about how easy it is to unsubscribe and how their e-mail will never be traded or given away blah blah blah. Now if this is where you stop, then you have not taken advantage of your autoresponder. An effective addition to your "thank you" e-mail might be to tell them about a special offer on one of your products and how it might benefit them. Perhaps a small image could be included with link to your sales letter. (html enhanced autoresponders are quite standard these days).

ex #2 A visitor subscribes to your *"free 7 day marketing e-course"*. Every day a time released autoresponder with a short article is sent out. Within each article, you have links to your affiliate products and ads to your own products. Kind of like a free eBook, but there is nothing to download.

ex #3 A visitor buys one of your products and gets a "thankyou" autoresponder. You might suggest another product, but as they have just purchased something from you, why not offer them a special client's discount and include a unique URL to that product? Specify the difference in price that a first time visitor would have to pay.

In all of these situations you can programme a few periodic *"how are you?"* autoresponders. If they subscribed to an e-course, then you might follow up with an autoresponder a couple of weeks later that says something like *"How did you enjoy the course? – can we also recommend blah blah blah"* etc.

Autoresponders are a way of building relationships with your clients. They are a way of reminding people about you, your products and services. It is very important that you do not abuse this promotional tool as I see many marketers do. They simply do not know when to stop. They assume that selling is just a numbers game, and of course they may be right, but I also think a degree of integrity is in order. An onslaught of popups and autoresponder bombardments simply tells me that they don't care about me. Do they need to care about me? Yes, if they want my business.

Offering your own affiliate programme

There are several marketers who rely almost 100% on their affiliates bringing in business for them. The "super affiliates" are clearly who they should be targeting and there is even software available to help find these. I can't recommend anything in particular, however, as I have not tried any yet. Feel free to do a *Google* search on *"find super affiliates"* and download some trial software. I must say, I personally don't believe one needs software to find super affiliates. Today, a super affiliate is nothing more than a very successful website, marketing products in a similar demographic to yours. You can find these websites usually quite easily by doing web searches. Simply contact the owner and request that they do a joint venture with you.

If you have a marketable product, you should invite affiliates to sell your product for a commission. I like to give 40% commission and give incentive to a few who know how to market successfully. The *1ShoppingCart* solution has a built in affiliate programme that makes the whole process nice and easy. Potential affiliates can sign up within 30 seconds and an autoresponder will hit them back immediately with their own unique URL. Anytime they direct visitors to your website, that unique URL is tracked and a "commissions payable" report is generated. Once a month you run a commissions payable report and write cheques to your affiliates. You can offer them banner or text links or both, in order to promote your products. All this is built in to the programme.

The affiliate programme will also generate an e-mail and send it to the affiliate every time he or she makes a sale. It is 100% automated. The only work involved for you on a continuous basis is writing the monthly cheques to your affiliates. Frankly if they are making sales for you, there is every incentive to do this.

When you offer an affiliate programme you will have various people signing up once in a while. Most of these folks have no clue about marketing online and only a very small percentage of these people will make sales for you. If you want affiliates to come through, you will need to approach the super affiliates yourself. Hunt them down through other successful competitive sites. They are out there. Go get 'em!

**You must make it clear to your affiliates
that *in no way* will you tolerate spam!**

You know those dull e-mails you get every day inviting you to enlarge your member, or buy Viagra, or purchase tooth whitening? Painful aren't they? Well they are all affiliates who are throwing mud at the wall hoping to make a quick buck and move on. This is not the way to market affiliate products and will only get YOU in trouble, if your own affiliates market your product this way. Make sure you add a warning followed by a sign-up autoresponder letting affiliates know that you will not tolerate this. Say something like:

WARNING: We will Not Tolerate Any Type Of Spam Or Bulk E-mail. DO NOT send unsolicited e-mail to promote us, or you will be in violation of your affiliates agreement and your account will be terminated, forfeiting all outstanding referral fees. Your cooperation and understanding is very much appreciated.

That should do it. Bear in mind that the super affiliates know what they are doing. For the most part, they will be using safe methods that actually do work.

Another excellent affiliate tracking programme, possibly the best on the market, is *AssocTRAC* (**www.marketingtips.com/assoctrac**). If you have already got your shopping cart and merchant account installed, and just want a dedicated affiliate tracking module, this is the way to go. You could also partner with a website that specializes in affiliate promotions and have an instant network promoting your digital products. One such company is *ClickBank* (**www.clickbank.com**) Other reputable organizations are *Shareasale* (**www.shareasale.com**) and *SellShareware.com* (**www.sellshareware.com**).

Managing mail lists and broadcasting

It has taken me a long time to learn the best way to manage an opt in subscriber list and I still haven't arrived at the absolute 100% perfect solution (not sure there is one) but I know the advantages and disadvantages of all the options now. I'll briefly go over the main issues so you can weigh up what will work best for you.

Once you get a substantial subscriber base, let's say over 2000 you cannot rely on simple e-mail broadcasting via your ISP e-mail client. All ISPs such as *AOL, Earthlink, MSN* and so on now have very strict rules regarding how many e-mails you can send out in a mailing list at one time. More than that, you really need to personalize each e-mail you send to a subscriber or client. Simply to start an e-mail with "Hello" or "Dear sir" is a little spammy, especially if the subscriber forgets he subscribed (happens all the time!). So, the first thing we need to talk about is the best way to collect and store contact data.

E-mail filtering

You need a system that will interact with your e-mail client and read web form submissions. For instance, when a subscriber signs up for your monthly newsletter, his contact info will be submitted to a specified e-mail account. Now, the old school method would have been to manually copy and paste the received e-mail into a database. Nowadays we can automate, rendering the primitive manual method unacceptable. The web form data will look like this, depending on what fields you specify in your web form:

firstname: Buffy
lastname: Brothspoiler
email: buffy@buffybrothspoiler.com
location: UK

Let's say you have a company called **www.yoga-news.com** You could set up a dedicated e-mail account, such as **subscribers@yoga-news.com** You assign your web form to submit its information to this e-mail address. (Remember we talked about hidden fields and **FormMail.cgi** scripts a while back?) The mail filter then interacts with that e-mail account and stores the information in a text file. You can then autorespond to the subscriber with a login & password, or a simple thankyou and so on, whatever the deal. Here are two excellent ways to filter your e-mail:

- **1ShoppingCart** (www.1shoppingcart.com)

  The *1ShoppingCart* complete E-Commerce solution has basic e-mail filtering built into its system, certainly as far as interacting with web forms are concerned. It allows you to subscribe and unsubscribe automatically. Because it offers the advantage of a shopping cart, merchant account, built in affiliate programme, web form template and bulk mail facility, this is an excellent choice, especially if you are fairly new to this.

- **Mailloop** (www.mailloop.com)

  Mailloop pretty much runs my online business and I can't say enough about it. I use both *1Shopping Cart* and Mailloop together. Although not totally complementary, I use them to do different things. Mailloop's e-mail filtering is without question the best I have ever seen. It will collect subscriber data, automatically unsubscribe at client's request, store data to list files, autorespond, redirect e-mail messages, delete messages from server and play a sound. (This is fun when you sell a product!). What I like about Mailloop is that the software sits on your computer hard drive. I can physically see the contact data as it comes in if I want. It's very hands-on in a way that storing data online isn't.

Broadcasting to your mail list

There are three ways to send bulk mail:

1) Through an online server/E-Commerce programme such as *1ShoppingCart.com*.
2) Through an independent online server specializing in newsletter broadcasting.
3) Using bulk mail software that you install on your computer, such as *Mailloop*.

Sending bulk mail using an online server

Using an online server has advantages and disadvantages. The advantage is that you can schedule a broadcast and get on with other things, assuming all goes well with the broadcast. The disadvantage is that you cannot really monitor the success of the broadcast. Sometimes servers go down and mail does not get sent. You have to trust that the system works. I used an independent company to send out my mail for a while and I was convinced that half of my subscribers were not receiving e-mails. Furthermore, my subscriber rate improved ten-fold when I changed over to my new system. Bizarre! I did not receive the "bounce backs", you know all the mailer daemons that inevitably happen when you send out to a large list, so I could not measure the success of the broadcast. Later on I purchased *Mailloop* for its many features, but of course an offline bulk mailer has its own set of issues. Let's talk about them, as this is extremely important stuff to know about if you intend to broadcast to a list.

Sending bulk mail is something that needs to be studied a little. You cannot simply buy software and just send tons of mail out. Most ISPs frown upon bulk mail as they are cautious of spam, and rightly so. They do not want people using their mail servers, upsetting people who haven't personally subscribed to a list. Whether you are actually spamming or legitimately sending newsletters to opt-in subscribers, the very fact that you are sending that much mail out at one time will inevitably cause anger from one or two individuals. Perhaps they forgot they subscribed. Who knows? It happens all the time.

If you decide to use an online broadcast server, my first choice would be *1ShoppingCart* because it includes a complete E-Commerce package and is extremely cost effective. If you already have a merchant account and shopping cart solution and just want a broadcast method, you might look into *GroupMail* (**www.group-mail.com**) by *Infacta Ltd*. Another excellent one is *Dada Mail* (**http://mojo.skazat.com**), or *AWeber* (**www.aweber.com**) which also has a first rate reputation.

Sending bulk mail using an offline mailer programme

In order to send bulk mail using software on your hard drive, you need to have access to a mail server. This is considered the legitimate way to broadcast and any web host will provide this access. This transfer method is called SMTP and stands for "Simple Mail Transport Protocol". In order to get over this first hump, it is important to make sure that the mail server you are using allows you to send to a large list. Some ISPs have a limit of say 50 e-mails that you can send out at one time. This, of course, is no good at all. Your web host should allow you to send large amounts of mail. Before you configure your bulk mail software, you might want to check with your ISP or web host that you are allowed to send out bulk mail. Find out what their limitations are. Explain that you have an opt-in list only (which you should have!).

Most of these bulk mail software programmes are designed with a built in SMTP server because the software designers know about this problem. (That and the fact that the companies are also marketing to spammers, even though they would never admit it.) What this means is that you can technically send out a large amount of mail using their software with the *"Act Like A Mail Server"* box checked. This way, the broadcast does not go through an external mail server and of course is very powerful because it just keeps running and running.

OK, here's the problem with this. A few of the larger ISPs such as *Earthlink, AOL* and *MSN* are completely hip to this and have decided to block e-mails that don't run smoothly through a legitimate, established SMTP server with a recognizable IP address. That means that quite possibly a third of your list won't receive their e-mails, if you decide to send your list using this method. Ludicrous! In my view, the *only* way to send bulk mail is through an SMTP server that allows you to do so. There are tons that do, trust me. Make sure you have this sorted out, or I guarantee frustration. Running a bulk mailer through SMTP is the way. That said, once in a while the mail server you are running through may go down, refuses access or assumes you are sending too much e-mail and so on. Because this happens from time to time, your broadcast needs to be monitored. Thankfully, your log and fail files can tell you at what point the broadcast failed so you can start a new mail-out. These problems happen more commonly when a server is busy with lots of traffic. A good time to send a mail out might be at night time when things are a little quieter.

Let's say you have a website at **www.real-estate-turkeys.co.uk** and you decide to use your web host's SMTP server to send your mailing. Provided you meet all the rules of your web host, all should go smoothly. However, don't forget that your ISP (the company that provides you with your internet connection, and probably separate from your web host) is monitoring you behind the scenes. Most ISPs now insist that you send mail through their server only. This, however, is no good to you because you need to be able to send out to a large list. Before you send out your first broadcast, you may need to contact your ISP and request that they "unblock port 25". This will remove your restriction and will allow you to send your mail through a third party server. Now, do bear in mind that once in a while if there is ever a problem, or a complaint from a subscriber, your ISP may automatically block port 25. Once in a while you may have to call them and lift the restriction. Sometimes a bit of a drag but provided you insist that you have an opt-in subscriber list, they should honour your request every time.

So which is best, online broadcasting or offline? Difficult to say. Personally the *absolute perfect* solution might be to own your own server where you personally administer the mail rules and then run a programme like *Mailloop* through it. This, of course, is pricey and a bit of a job to set up. At some point I will do this, especially when my lists get totally out of hand. You would do well to establish a personal relationship with a web host and explain that you need them to work with you on this solution. In the beginning while your lists are small, you could go either way. When they get up over the 10,000 mark, then you need to reevaluate.

One important point if you are going to talk to a web host about this: most hosting companies are in fierce competition with each other and simply want your business. Most of the "tech support" guys are not that technical and generally the sales guys are simply trained to make a sale and are not technical in any way. My point is that you simply *have* to talk with someone who knows about the company's mail server rules before you go ahead and purchase web hosting. I would hate for you to send your first mail out and have access denied after just 300 e-mails sent.

Finally, I would probably give a big thumbs up to *Mailloop* because it has a list processor. This is worth the price of the programme in itself. When you have a mail list, you will inevitably find that subscribers submit more than once, often through no fault of their own. Subscribers enter e-mail addresses that don't mean anything, such as **www.me@mysite.net** or an address without the @ included or just complete nonsense. I see this daily. Lists need to be cleaned to weed out the rubbish. An online server has a somewhat efficient automated clean up system but never that great. Mailloop's list filter does this amazingly. It will also return a list of fields that you specify. For instance, you can ask it to return a list with **AOL.com** subscribers only, or subscribers that live in Yorkshire [location] only, or whatever field name you specify. You can subtract a list within a list and so on.

Smart marketing ideas

Let's talk about ways other than page optimization that will help generate a steady flow of traffic to your website.

Affiliate programmes

We have talked briefly about affiliate programmes. You should be affiliated with other products so you can make extra money and you should have your own affiliate programme so others can sell your products. Let's talk a little more about affiliating with *other* people's products.

Most folks think that placing a banner on their website, linking to an affiliate product will make them money. Whilst occasionally this works, for the most part it does not. Of course, it is a numbers game and the more traffic you get to your web page the more likely it is that someone will step through to your affiliate link. There are a few effective ways to sell affiliate products. Number one rule of thumb:

Only sell affiliate products that are relevant to your readers!

On my music site at **www.aandronline.com** I sell several affiliate products very successfully. As the site is geared to independent and unsigned artists, it makes sense to offer products musicians can use to get to the next rung of the ladder in a highly competitive business. One of the products is the *A&R Registry* (**www.aandronline.com/music-registry**), a database of thousands of music industry contacts. This has been professionally put together and is a wonderful resource for musicians. The product sells daily and I get a healthy 40% commission. I also sell other authors' "how to" eBooks and so on. They sell from the site because they are 100% relevant to my readers.

Now, I also sell the same affiliate products in my fortnightly newsletter that goes out to subscribers. Once in a while, if I have a new affiliate product that I think will do well, I will send out a dedicated e-blast highly recommending it.

The key to selling affiliate products successfully via e-mail is
Personal recommendation!

Your readers will have, over the months and years, built up a trust and confidence in you and will listen to your expertise. You can take advantage of this by direct marketing to them. A dedicated e-blast recommending an affiliate product is an extremely effective way to go.

If you are offering an affiliate product that is extremely popular on many websites, you should ask yourself a very important question: *"Why should people buy from me instead of anywhere else?"* This one question is guaranteed to increase your sales dramatically. If you sell an affiliate product, then giving away something of value along with it might be effective. For example, suppose you are looking to buy a new car. You even know the exact car you want to buy. You go around several car dealers and the prices are the same. However, one dealer offers you a huge incentive - a year's supply of free gas! Clearly you would go to the dealer that adds more value to your deal. Affiliate programmes are a little bit like this example because the product owner sets the price. Then it's down to how smart the affiliate can be to sell the product. So the simple answer to successful affiliate marketing is this: *Offer more!*

The obvious incentive that comes to mind is including a free eBook, but I suggest you get a little more creative. If you are a good web designer and your website is related to graphics, maybe give away a set of html templates, maybe some eBook cover templates that users can simply add the name of their product to. You could even offer free advertising for a week on your site to anyone who buys from you. You could dedicate a web page to do this alone and update it regularly. Make sure it is linked clearly from your home page with a clear incentive for visitors to go there. You could also offer free advertising space in your newsletter (if your affiliate commission justified it). Perhaps one of your affiliate products is a piece of software that you personally use and that you recommend highly. Perhaps installing and setting up this software in order for it to run smoothly takes a bit of work. Many folks aren't that technically minded so your sale incentive might be to set the software up for them. This, of course, is physically time consuming and something I would rather avoid, so here is a better idea to ponder:

How many times have you bought software and despite reading through the manual, found several major issues that are not addressed or explained thoroughly? What if you became an expert using this programme and devised several tips and tricks to get round these problems? If this is the case, you should write your own downloadable document that outlines all these points, kind of like a manual or expert's handbook. You simply include this as your bonus incentive. Anybody else doing this? Probably not. *You* get the edge. You might even consider converting the handbook to a simple html web page and propose that the manufacturer's website links to it. They might appreciate this and send traffic your way enabling visitors to buy through your affiliate link!

Put your thinking cap on. Challenge yourself for ideas. I like to go for long walks alone and figure stuff like this out in my head. Generally, by the time I get home, I have a germ of a plan.

Try before you buy

Clearly this is a good incentive to offer if you are selling a programme. eBooks are not really conducive to this idea (a money back guarantee is better). Of course, some of your affiliate programmes will offer a "try before you buy" incentive and you can mention this in your own newsletters/ads etc.

Discounts on larger purchases

I like to offer discounts to buyers when they spend more. The more they spend the bigger the discount. You can configure this in your shopping cart. A very basic version of this might be an "upsell" page that readers step through from a sales letter "buy me" link. Instead of going straight to the order page, they are prompted to choose whether they want to add an extra discounted product or simply order just the one product. You can see an example of this on the next page.

Syndicating articles

If you write articles for your own newsletter, you should consider syndicating them to other websites. Standard practice is that no money changes hands, but there is a fair exchange. Every article you submit contains a link and description back to your own site. I do this and have built up quite a number of ezines that display my articles. It's a great way to build your perception of expertise and get traffic. I even make it easy for other ezines to subscribe to my *"article syndication mail list"*. I simply add a subscribe link at the bottom of each article. My e-mail filter then stores the mail merged info and any time I write a new article, I send out a newsletter to that list. This is a very powerful marketing tool and if you enjoy writing, then this is to be highly recommended. Check out *IdeaMarketers* (www.ideamarketers.com) to look into this further.

It is entirely possible that writing articles is becoming the very best way to get high search engine results. Recent studies have shown that *Google* may be looking much more seriously at one-way links. In other words, even though reciprocal linking is extremely important, an inbound link without an outbound link from your site shows that your site is more relevant to Google. This theory is being put to the test now. With this in mind, providing articles of expertise on other sites, with a link back to your site will generate one way links. I highly recommend this form of online promotion.

Displaying articles on your site written by others

If you syndicate your articles to others you might also display articles on your website written by other experts in your field. It is always good to get another expert's perspective. Propose this idea to other sites and make it clear on your site that you are interested in doing this. If you have a popular site, you will receive a number of proposals. Check out **www.ezinearticles.com** if you are looking for content.

Advertising offline

Traditional advertising in magazines (that you might buy from a newsstand) is a good form of name branding but might not necessarily lead directly to sales. Promoting online is more effective because you can take advantage of the impulse buyer. Just a few steps can get a buyer to the order page for an immediate sale. Reading a magazine does not present such an immediate call to action. With this in mind, I do recommend traditional advertising for your website, but understand that your advertisement must create a reason for readers to put down the magazine and go to the computer. Bear in mind that they might be sitting on a bus or a train so the impact of your ad must be strong enough to stay with them. A contest or some incentive to subscribe is always good. Remember, once you have their e-mail address, you can market directly so offering huge incentives to subscribe might work. Give it some serious thought. Aside from that, simple name branding *is* a justifiable reason to advertise. I like long term goal setting as well as short term.

Reselling your product

Some websites don't want to enter into a simple affiliate programme with you. They want to sell your product from their site and do fulfillment their end. In the case of an eBook they want to take 50% commission and take care of downloads. Bigger sites have the clout to pull this off because of high traffic and you should take advantage of this even though you are forfeiting a larger commission. The point is, this isn't going to hurt you in any way. I used to think that if a competitive site sold my eBook then it would take away sales from my website. Not so. It's a little bit like having the same book in several bookstores. An external website will have its own demographic, its own subscriber list it can sell to, and its own board of "experts" that its audience looks up to. You have your own. All you are doing by offering your book to resellers is making more money. Another monthly cheque wouldn't hurt would it? The downside to this is that there are usually no stats to login to like there are on an affiliate programme, you simply trust that the monthly cheque they send you actually represents sales. You can either propose reselling to your competitors or make it known on your site that you are interested in talking about resell rights regarding your own products. Preferably both.

Accepting paid advertising from third parties

Once your subscriber list hits 10,000 you can legitimately accept paid advertising from third parties in your newsletter. If you get over 500 unique targeted visitors per day, you could also place ads on your most populated web page (presumably index page). Your advertising price should be proportional to the amount of subscribers & traffic you have. You could offer two services and variations thereof:

1) Advertising placement within newsletter

A very cost effective way for a third party to advertise is by placing an ad in someone else's newsletter. It introduces them to a whole new audience and can be very effective. Placement within the newsletter is key so you might offer two or three placement options, top of page being most expensive.

2) Stand alone dedicated e-blast

This is clearly the most effective way for an external website to advertise using your subscriber mailing list. You send an e-blast advertisement about a third party product to your subscribers. However, this is somewhat risky for you because your subscribers may feel a little cheated or spammed. The way to get round this is to add a short paragraph to personally recommend the product. This form of advertising should clearly be the most expensive as you run the risk of losing subscribers.

Advertising your product on external sites

The two above ideas can be turned around, so effectively *you* are the advertiser. If you come across very popular sites that have a similar audience to yours, then you should consider advertising with them. Most sites are looking for ways to make revenue and advertising is usually welcomed with open arms.

Newsletter ad trades

If you have a relationship with a competitor site, you might propose the idea of a newsletter ad trade. You simply both place an ad in each other's newsletter and no money needs to exchange hands. The question of *who has the most subscribers* will inevitably come up. If you both have roughly the same, give or take a couple of thousand, I would say this is grounds for a straight trade. If there is a gap of several thousands, then you may have to negotiate a little. If your partner site has more than you, you could always offer them an additional ad on your most visited web page for X number of days. Get creative. These things can always be worked out if there is something in it for all concerned.

Pay per click promotion

I talked about *Overture* in the first half of this book. Refer to this section again, as this might be worth the investment.

Joint ventures

I get e-mails on a regular basis from other websites proposing to work together. Mostly these sites have a similar demographic and feel there is a way to work together. The e-mails very often say something like:

"Because our sites target a similar audience, I feel that working together would mutually benefit us. Perhaps there is some way we can do this. Please call me so we can discuss some ideas".

I find these e-mails just a little annoying. Why? Because it seems like there has been no effort gone into thinking about **how** we might benefit each other. It's like saying "I can't think of anything perhaps *you* can!" Now don't get me wrong, there is every likelihood that we *could* benefit from working together and I am always open to ideas, but for Pete's sake give me a clue!! Put a proposal forward and let me spark off that. Otherwise, you are asking me to come up with ideas to make your website successful and frankly I don't have time.

If you have an online business that might complement another, then put a simple proposal together, send an e-mail or make a phone call. If you have something that will obviously benefit another, then I guarantee they will come forward and respond. Cross promotion is a very powerful marketing tool and can double your traffic if the model is sound.

Promoting yourself as a celebrity

Finally, I want to talk about a whole different aspect of promotion on the Internet. So far, we have talked about promoting products and services on the Internet, essentially things that directly benefit the consumer. We can sell these things successfully because we can market them as things that consumers need. Anytime someone is searching for something online, then the theory holds that these folks can be marketed to. What I want to talk about now is how *individuals* can be promoted online. You know, people who are forging a path as artists or entertainers of some sort. These folks are the product themselves to a degree. Although a musician may have a CD to sell, he is in effect promoting himself as a product. The CD is just a by-product of himself. Similarly, an actor only has himself to promote. He *is* his product.

> ## We need to differentiate between a *subjective* product and an *objective* one.

Let's look at it another way: a company selling baked beans is promoting an objective product because it's all about the can of beans. Nobody cares two hoots about the CEO. A saxophone player on the other hand is a subjective product. If he or she wants work, they need to get on the phone and ostensibly say "Book me, I'm worth it!" It's a whole different sales mentality (which is probably why there are so many neurotic artists!). I want to address this subjective product marketing angle because the Internet is rife with folks trying to promote their own individual names. The trouble is that it's the marketers selling objective products who are making the dough. Entertainers are doing a pitiful job and there is a simple explanation why:

> ## Products sell on the Internet when they provide a direct benefit to the consumer!

A musician searching for information on *"How to make a winning press kit so record companies pay attention"* can be marketed to. There is a direct benefit for that musician. There is something in it for *him*. Now for example, if you are part of a new band called "Johnny Crimble and the Birthday Cakes", you put up a website with all the glitz and glamour you can muster and you link to other relevant websites, how successful do you think you would be? You even have a page rank of 5/10 because of your linking strategy. How many CDs do you think you would sell? Let's say you adopt all the principles of this course. Well, if you promote correctly you will get some traffic and make a few sales. The truth of the matter is you will probably be disappointed. Why? Because nobody is searching for you! Go to the *Overture* search engine suggestion tool (**http://inventory.overture.com/d/searchinventory/suggestion**) and type in "Johnny Crimble and the Birthday Cakes" or any other new unsigned band for that matter. No one is searching. Why? Because they don't already know about you! You can't blame them though. After all, how can they do a search on you if they haven't already heard about you, or seen you play at a show? Even if they have heard about you, the problem is that there is no direct benefit to help them in their plight to success.

Entertainment is a *want* not a *need!*

The benefit lies with the musician selling the CD, not the recipient. Now, if a fan saw a live show, loved it and couldn't buy their CD at a show, couldn't find it in a store, then and only then might they do a search and end up at your website. Doesn't look rosy does it?

So whether you are an actor, a comedian, musician or any kind of entertainer attempting to promote yourself on the Internet, the question to ask yourself is *"How can I get people to discover me?"* or more appropriately *"Where are my potential fans hanging out?"*. Hmmm. I like this last question. Let's explore it a little.

Let's say your band *Johnny Crimble and the Birthday Cakes* is on the scene gigging at clubs a couple of times a month, trying desperately to get attention from the music big wigs. What if all of a sudden you managed to get on a six week tour opening for a hugely successful band? Maybe the headlining band are heroes of yours. How would you feel if you got to open for them? Pretty good huh? The reasons you would be excited are:

1 you would get a huge amount of exposure from a whole new audience and
2) there is a similarity between the headliner's music and yours, and you feel certain that their fans would dig your music too!

And herein lies the answer to promoting individuals online. We are going to take this model and apply it to the Internet.

The most effective way to promote a subjective product online is by taking advantage of an already successful subjective product!

Let's assume you are a comedian. Your favourite stand up is Jack Dee. He's your biggest influence and frankly has a similar sense of humour to yours. Jack Dee is a household name in the UK and people do Internet searches on him daily, so you might ask yourself *"Where do fans of Jack Dee hang out so I can somehow grab them and make them mine?"*. Well, you can do your own search and might discover a few websites dedicated to him. You could even try and propose a feature all about you in an ezine dedicated to comedians. This is still hard because you have to sell yourself, just like hustling a gig.

The most powerful thing you could do is to start a website yourself dedicated to Jack Dee and other well known comedians. Essentially you promote your very own ezine where you discuss the art of stand up comedy, interview comedians and even sell DVDs and audio albums through affiliate links etc.

And here's where it gets really cool: you adopt every single principle I have told you in this handbook and you create a huge traffic jam to your website. Now you can take advantage of your 100% targeted audience. You feature yourself throughout the website, seduce folks using buzzword headings, and they can read all about you on a web page dedicated to just *you!* You promote your gig schedule, display a short interview, include some photos and you even ace it by adding audio featuring a 10 minute stand up routine. Now you've got 'em using the ultimate pull technique. You don't have to go begging to other ezines. They are coming straight to you just like you wanted all along.

You are probably thinking this is all hard work right? Well no. No harder than promoting any other website. Again, once it is optimized and up and running, monthly updates may be all that is required. Link trades, maybe a newsletter visitors can subscribe to. This is really smart proactive marketing!

Let me show you a way I recently implemented this idea. As I have mentioned one or two times, I have a very popular website dedicated to jazz guitar enthusiasts at **www.PlayJazzGuitar.com**. The site is mostly geared to sell my home study course but whenever I have a new CD release of my own, it is a perfect platform. I'm a jazz guitarist after all. It occurred to me sometime ago that I could capitalize on all the targeted traffic I was getting and parlay that directly into record sales. I decided to make web pages dedicated to 16 of the most famous jazz guitarists that ever walked this earth. These people included Jim Hall, Pat Metheny, Wes Montgomery as well as more contemporary guys like John Scofield, Larry Carlton and Lee Ritenour. The whole idea was to make these pages search engine friendly so that whenever anyone searched on any of those names in *Google,* those artist pages at my website came up high in the results. Each page contained a photo, short historical bio and an affiliate link to **Amazon.com** directing visitors to buy that player's most popular CD. (OK *Amazon's* affiliate programme pays peanuts but I don't like to miss a trick!).

Now here's the marketing brilliance, even if I say so myself. On each player's web page I also included a short paragraph introducing my home study jazz guitar course. There is also a paragraph and seductive heading about my latest CD with a link to listen and buy. For the more contemporary players like George Benson and Pat Metheny, on their pages I added a timed popup page which opens after about 20 seconds that says *"If you like George Benson's music, you will most likely enjoy the latest album from guitarist Chris Standring".* Immediately there is an audio file that streams for about 30 seconds. From that popup, visitors can click through to my personal website, listen to more or buy through my credit card server. Ta - dah!!!!

Some visitors may find this to be aggressive marketing, but frankly the chances are they will like the music if they like the players I have associated my popups with. Perhaps John Scofield fans may be a little offended, as the music on my CDs is much more commercial and because of this, I refrained from adding the popup from his page (and a few others). The point is I am taking advantage of an existing audience that is right in the same ball park as mine and this is the secret to promoting new celebrities online.

This is a very advanced technique and depending on what field you are promoting, competitive keywords may well be a factor.

Actually, Amazon.com does a very similar thing but not quite as blatantly. Whenever you search for an artist, there is always a short list saying *"People who bought this record also bought this this and this"* along with links to buy those CDs. They have created a brilliant "related products" programme. It works purely because it is targeted.

So with that, if you aspire to be a celebrity and want to take advantage of the Internet simply ask *"Who is successful already that has an audience that would dig me?"*.

Final thought

Building a business online is a slow but sure process. It takes a good idea, commitment to hard work and a level of integrity for it all to come to fruition. This and the open mindedness to accept change will stand you in good stead. The Internet is moving at rapid speeds and it is important to stay on top. One thing I am sure of is that the world wide web isn't going away anytime soon. I believe we are still at the beginning – but it IS the future. Now is the perfect time to jump on board, put your business online and stay way ahead of the pack. Good luck and go get 'em!

Software and resources (recap)

Affiliate Programs

AssocTRAC Affiliate tracking software
www.marketingtips.com/assoctrac

ClickBank Affiliate product network
www.clickbank.com

Shareasale Affiliate product network
www.shareasale.com

SellShareware.com Affiliate product network
www.sellshareware.com

Audio

Audiograbber Extract and convert to MP3 or WAV
www.audiograbber.com-us.net

RealProducer Make RealAudio and RealVideo files
www.realnetworks.com/products/producer/basic.html

Sound Forge Edit audio files
www.sonymediasoftware.com/products

FlexiMusic Edit audio files
www.fleximusic.com

Codes & Scripts

You may have to view source to copy these codes

Matt Wright's script archive
www.scriptarchive.com

Download all the following javascripts in zip file:
www.aandronline.com/wps/scripts/javascripts.zip

Add bookmark Book marks web page
www.aandronline.com/wps/scripts/add_bookmark.txt

Auto popup Creates an auto popup
www.aandronline.com/wps/scripts/auto_pop_up.txt

Close window Close web page window
www.aandronline.com/wps/scripts/close_window.txt

Date Displays date
www.aandronline.com/wps/scripts/date.txt

Delayed popup Creates a timed popup
www.aandronline.com/wps/scripts/delayed_popup.txt

Disable right click Disallows view source
www.aandronline.com/wps/scripts/disable_right_click.txt

E-mail to friend #1 Tell a friend
www.aandronline.com/wps/scripts/email_2_friend.txt

E-mail to friend #2 Tell a friend
www.aandronline.com/wps/scripts/email_2_friend2.txt

Framebuster Opens a framed page to a new window
www.aandronline.com/wps/scripts/framebuster.txt

Highlight text Text highlighter
www.aandronline.com/wps/scripts/highlight_text.txt

Link on submit Sends to a designated URL from a submit button
www.aandronline.com/wps/scripts/link_on_submit.txt

Popup on submit Creates popup window from a submit button
www.aandronline.com/wps/scripts/pop_up_on_submit_button.txt

Popup on click Creates popup from a text hyperlink
www.aandronline.com/wps/scripts/popup_on_click.txt

Popup on leave Creates popup when browser closed out
www.aandronline.com/wps/scripts/popup_on_leave.txt

Popup once only Creates popup only once
www.aandronline.com/wps/scripts/popup_once.txt

Preload images Preloads images on web page
www.aandronline.com/wps/scripts/preload_images.txt

Scrollbar color change Add color to your scrollbar
www.aandronline.com/wps/scripts/scrollbar_color_change.txt

Statusbar message scrolls Add a scrollbar message when web page loads
www.aandronline.com/wps/scripts/statusbar_message_scrolls.txt

Title scroll Title scrolls
www.aandronline.com/wps/scripts/title_scroll.txt

Link proposal contact form Template form
www.aandronline.com/wps/scripts/link_proposal.html

eBooks

eBook Pro eBook creator software
www.ebookpro.com

eBookGold eBook creator software
www.ebookgold.com

Adobe Acrobat Software that makes pdf files
www.adobe.com

Adobe Reader Reads pdf files (free download)
www.adobe.com/products/acrobat/readstep2.html

Virtual Cover Creator eBook and box cover image creator
www.virtual-cover-creator.net

IdeaMarketers Share and find articles
www.ideamarketers.com

EzineArticles.com Free content for your site
www.ezinearticles.com

E-Commerce

1ShoppingCart.com Complete E-Commerce solution
www.1shoppingcart.com

Mailloop E-mail filtering/broadcasting/list processing
www.mailloop.com

Graphics & Design

Adobe Photoshop Industry standard photo, design and paint program
www.adobe.com

Paint Shop Pro A mini Photoshop
www.jasc.com

Flash Animation program
www.flash.com

HTML

Dreamweaver Professional html authoring software
www.macromedia.com

CoffeeCup HTML Editor Professional html authoring software
www.coffeecup.com

Learn HTML in a Weekend Handy book to have
www.amazon.com/books

CuteFTP Industry standard in file transfer protocol
www.cuteftp.com

WS_FTP Industry standard in file transfer protocol
www.wsftp.com

WebPosition Software that helps you optimize web pages
www.webposition.com

CoffeeCup Password Wizard Handy password protect
www.coffeecup.com

.htpasswd Encryption Tool Encrypt passwords for .htaccess
www.4webhelp.net/us/password.php

Linking

Google toolbar View external website's page rank
http://toolbar.google.com

ARELIS Reciprocal link trading solution
www.axandra.com

Alexa Get detailed stats on websites
www.alexa.com

Miscellaneous

TheCounter.com Affordable web counter with stats
www.thecounter.com

Digital Photos Screensaver Maker Create slideshows and screensavers
www.photos-screensaver-maker.com

InstantSalesLetters Help with sales letters
www.instantsalesletters.com

phpBB Free bulletin board
www.phpbb.com

Search Engines

SearchEngineWatch Keep up to date with all the latest changes
www.searchenginewatch.com

Atomz Add search engine to your web domain
www.atomz.com

Google Add URL:
www.google.com/addurl.html

Open Directory Add URL:
www.dmoz.org/add.html

Yahoo Add URL:
http://docs.yahoo.com/info/suggest

AOL.com Add URL: Via Google add URL
www.google.com/addurl.html

AltaVista Add URL:
http://addurl.altavista.com

Netscape Add URL: Via Google add URL
www.google.com/addurl.html

All The Web (Fast) Add URL:
www.alltheweb.com/help/webmaster/submit_site

Hotbot Add URL: Via Lycos add URL
http://insite.lycos.com

Lycos Add URL:
http://insite.lycos.com

Excite Add URL:
https://secure.ah-ha.com/guaranteed_inclusion/teaser.aspx

Looksmart Add URL:
http://listings.looksmart.com

MSN Add URL:
http://submitit.bcentral.com/msnsubmit.htm

Ask Jeeves Add URL:
http://ask.ineedhits.com/sitesubmit.asp?id=30129

Inktomi Add URL: Via MSN add URL
http://submitit.bcentral.com/msnsubmit.htm

Overture Pay per click
www.overture.com

FindWhat.com Pay per click
www.findwhat.com

Kanoodle Pay per click
www.kanoodle.com

Web Hosting

TotalChoiceHosting Affordable web hosting
www.totalchoicehosting.com

HostRocket.com Affordable web hosting
www.hostrocket.com